This book is dedicated to

my mother.

Sheryl Ann Carmichael.

Mama, I made it!

Psalms 23.

"Nothing can dim the light that shines from within."

- Maya Angelou

Acknowledgements

First, I wanna thank God for getting me through to complete this book. To my fiancé, Devon thank you for being my ear and pushing me to believe in myself. To my children Za'Mira, Zaire, and Za'Khari aka Z3Creationz thank you for understanding, allowing me the space and time to complete one of my goals. To my circle of sisters and brother, thank you for being my cheerleaders and encouraging me to release this book.

What About ME
Pt. 1

By: D. Carmichael

What About ME by D. Carmichael

Published by Desiree Carmichael

Copyright © 2024 D. Carmichael

All rights reserved. No portion of this book may be reproduced in any form without prior permission from the copyright owner of this book.

ISBN: 979-8-218-51348-1

Chapter 1
Whatever That Means

Just got off the bus from school and was greeted by my best friend Serenity. She is homeschooled cause her dad slept with half the teachers at her school. Her mom said it's because of the school curriculum but we know the real reason why. She doesn't want Serenity to be bullied because of her dad. She goes to a Catholic School in our town. "Hey girl is you staying outside to play with us?" "Let me check on Robbie first, you know it's the 2nd and sometimes my parents fight".

I enter the house, hear glass hit the wall, and break. I look to the left and Robbie is under the table. That is our safe space when our parents are fighting nothing can touch us under there. I hang my bookbag on the coat rack and join Robbie under the table. He doesn't like noise, so he is covering his ears. About 5 mins later the door slams. My dad must have left, and the coast was clear. My mom's face was swollen, and her lip was bleeding. Robbie began to clean up the glass. I went into the kitchen, got a bowl of warm water and 2 towels. We were running out of towels because the other ones were so bloody; we threw them out.

Mama snatched the wet towel from me and put it to her lip. "You know if your check comes on time this wouldn't happen. This is your fault." Every month mama and daddy get a check for me and Robbie. Daddy said it's because I get straight A's and have perfect attendance.

He said Robbie is so smart with building things the school rewards mama and daddy with a check to show their appreciation about how great parents mama and daddy were. "I need more make up because I am running low." Mama is always buying new makeup. She doesn't really go out in public, so I don't understand why she is always needing makeup.

An hour later daddy walks in the door with envelopes in his hands. The mailman must have come. Daddy yells out "Who wants ice cream?" I jump up and down and say "Me, me, me" Robbie wasn't as excited as me. We walked to the corner store to get some ice cream. Daddy said Dairy Queen and Rita's was too expensive and we couldn't afford it. Robbie picks up a snow cone and I said "Eww that is basically water." Robbie said, "When I get home, I pour sugar on it to make it sweet." I pretended to throw up and proceeded to grab my Chocolate Éclair.

Mama was trying to get daddy attention, but he was talking to the lady behind the counter. Well talking to her breast, I should say because that's all you can focus on. They were practically sitting on the counter. Daddy handed her $2 and told her to keep the change. When we got back home Serenity ran up to me. "Hey girl Jane said she want to battle you in jump rope." Now I don't know why she even playing with me like that. She keeps coming back to battle me and gets beat every time. "Mama, can I stay outside and play please?" Daddy said, "Go ahead pumpkin you made up for a great day." Whatever that means. "Yay, thanks daddy!"

"10,20,30,40,50,60,70,80,90 1 up, 2 up." I have been jumping for 2 mins straight to beat my old record of 4 mins and 30 seconds. Jane standing there just waiting for me to mess up. I blew her a kiss as I was doing my turns. "C'mon girl my arms hurt; you already beat Jane time of 30 seconds," cried Rebecca. "Stop complaining and just turn. I am trying to beat my old record." "Serenity let's go" yelled Serenity's mother. The streetlights were on so that meant it was time for us all to go home. "Whew thank God saved by the streetlights," said Rebecca. She turned collapsy anyway, I always have to talk to her while I am jumping. I stopped jumping and said "Aight y'all same time and place tomorrow. I'm out a sista is hungry."

We looked across the street while a Uhaul pulls into the driveway. A woman, her husband (I assume), son, and twin daughters jump out the car behind the truck. "Ahh more new people on the block?" Jane whined. "Girl you been here 6 months and still on friend probation. Who are you to talk?" said Serenity. We all chuckled and went our separate ways. I looked back, the boy and I locked eyes. I

shut the door behind me, last thing I need
is for daddy to see me looking at some
boy. A no good for nothing pissy boy as he
would say.

After I ate dinner and showered, I
peeked out the window to see if they
were still moving things in. I never even
seen a for sale/rent sign, I just knew the
old mean lady died. Her daughter
cremated her and poured her ashes in a
bon fire. She said she can burn 3x, while
getting cremated, at the bon fire and in
hell. It was too dark to really see
anything, so I turned my tv on. I have a

box tv that only plays in black and white. I love being at Serenity house she has all color TVs and cable. Sometimes her mom would say "All that money they get for you and y'all aint got no cable or color TVs." I told her I've been doing good in school, so the checks won't stop coming. She laughed and said, "That's what your folks told you?" and walked away. Whatever that means. Daddy said we can't afford cable, so we only have channels, 2,4,7,9,11, and 13.

Robbie is in his room probably building something. He doesn't like to come outside and play. He likes to build things like cars, airplanes etc. Sometimes he takes them apart and put them back together, I'm talking over 500 pieces sometimes. I turn to channel 13 and watch Arthur. Periodically I hit the side of my tv to make sure it plays right. I couldn't have a sister like DW. I am so glad Robbie is so cool and calm. He doesn't like to be put on the spot, he stays to himself and out of trouble.

Unlike Janes brother who has been suspended 4x and they only moved here 6 months ago. According to Jordan some kid was talking smack on the PlayStation, so he had to handle him in school. One day when I get a job, I will buy a color tv and have cable. I asked mama if we can get 1 for Christmas this year. I mean it's only June we have time to save up. But she said daddy handles the money and said we can't afford it. She said she will speak with my case worker cause Robbie, and I are eating up too much food and the money isn't enough. I have a school counselor at school not a case worker, *whatever that means.*

Chapter 2
Well Ok

Today is the last day of school and 7th grade has been so easy. I always try to make my daddy proud. He says we need the money so I can't mess it up. "Good morning mama" I said. "Hey child, hurry up and eat. The bus will be here soon" mama said. I still have about 15 minutes before the bus comes. I wasn't hungry from all the excitement of getting to school. Today we get our report cards, and we will know who our 8th grade teachers are. I wonder if the boy across the street will be going to my school. Speaking of, I am going to see if I can catch him outside leaving or something. "Bye mama I'm going to the bus stop" I yelled as I closed the door and rushed down the steps. I got outside and the Uhaul was gone. Instead, there was a Honda Accord Ex in the driveway. I walked to the bus stop and saw daddy coming out of the store with a big ol grin on his face. Must have seen the breast lady again.

"Quiet down class, I don't care if it's the last day. Act like y'all got some sense." That was our teacher Mrs. Treeburn. She could be a buzz kill sometimes. But I stay on her good side. Daddy said he better not ever get a call from school saying I was acting up. Mama said she would come and beat me in front of the class. "Yeah, and the checks would stop coming. We don't need that" daddy chimed in. So, every year I ask to sit in the front of the class. Front row right in the center. Too much happens in the back of the class, and I don't want no parts of it.

"Ok I am giving out report cards now so find y'all correct seats, or no one gets them." Typical Mrs. Treeburn always making the entire class suffer because of 1 or 2 people. I was so anxious to find out who my teacher was for 8th grade and if any of my friends were going to be in my class. I really wish Serenity went to school with me. Mama and daddy don't allow me to use the house phone. So, I only see Serenity when we are outside playing, or I go over to her house. Mama allows me to go when daddy isn't home. He doesn't like Serenity's mom and thinks she tells everyone's business.

"I don't need her to be around that chatter box. The wrong thing will slip out." I overheard daddy telling mama one night after I came inside from being at Serenity's house. I don't know what there is to tell. I mean we are not an exciting family at all, but I shrugged my shoulders and said well ok. Daddy knocked on my door "Listen pumpkin, I like Serenity but her mama not so much. I want you around good role model adults like me and mama, ok?" I said, "sure daddy ok."

Jane sits down in the seat next to me and asked me who my teacher was. I opened my report card and didn't look at my grades, I already knew that outcome. I look to the bottom right corner, and it says *94-95 8th grade school year teacher Mrs. BlueBridge.* "We are in the same class again" Jane says in excitement. I said "Yeah but who is she? There is no teacher here by that name." She must be new, and I don't like new teachers. All the teachers here know me and my family. They know I must get good grades. Now I have to get to know a whole new person.

I see Rebecca at the lunch table, and she says she has Mr. Ford aka Mr. Fraud. That's the teacher everyone wants because rumor has it, he takes it easy on 8th graders. He says high school is hard enough why stress your 8th grade year. It would be nice to have him so I can study less. In the beginning of the school year, I am not allowed outside afterschool. Daddy says I have to buckle down and learn the new grade so I can do good. Mama says that's what the teachers are for. Daddy shot her a look and said, "Well do you want the checks to stop?" Mama put her head down and said no. I just say well ok and go into my room.

I am going to have so much fun this summer because once the first day of school comes it is crunch time. But in the meantime, I need to find out who Mrs. BlueBridge is. The table next to us was so loud, I couldn't hear myself think to come up with a plan to find this new teacher. They were playing spoons. Being that it was the last day of school the winner just wanted bragging rights throughout the summer. Today's lunch was pizza and chocolate milk. I love school pizza, but I bring the milk home. Sometimes when the milk goes bad at home it's because daddy didn't buy any and he's usually gone for 2-3 days. Mama says she doesn't have any money so she can't go to the store. Robbie loves the chocolate milk, so I let him have it. Rebecca and Jane give me their milk too if they don't drink it. Today is the last day for me to stack up on as much milk as possible. I don't know what we are going to do during this summer break.

"Hey Ms. Arnold, is there any leftover milk?" Ms. Arnold giggled "I was waiting for you to come ask. There is actually a whole crate leftover, but it is too much for you to carry. I will drop it off to your house later after school." I started jumping up and down shouting "Thank you so much Ms. Arnold! Robbie is going to be so happy!" "Tell him don't drink it all at once ya hear?" Ms. Arnold is our head lunch lady. 7th and 8th graders go to lunch last, and she normally starts counting inventory for the next day. Sometimes I am lucky and get 2 extra milks to take home to Robbie. Ms. Arnold goes to church down the street from my house.

She always gives us peppermints or these strawberry candies. One time she invited all of us kids on the block to go to church with her. She said its no excuse to not praise God. If you can get up on Saturday morning and watch cartoons with your soggy cereal. You can do it again on Sunday. Jane said church is just too long and then they want you to go to evening services. I told Ms. Arnold I needed to be in bed by a certain time to get ready for school. She chuckled and said "Y'all can at least go to Sunday School." Daddy said God isn't real, he is my God and he saved me. I looked at him and said well ok. Ms. Arnold said, "Chile that no good daddy of yours don't know nothing about my God." Rebecca said "Oooo Ms. Arnold you are talking bad about your brother in Christ." Ms. Arnold told Rebecca to stay in a child's place.

We all chuckled and went back to playing jump rope. "Ok chile I will be there by 4:00 to drop off the milk." "Ok I'll be home and so will Robbie." "You coming to church Sunday" asked Ms. Arnold. "I will have to ask my mama and daddy." "Well let me know, I saw this nice dress and socks you can wear." She looked me up and down "Yeah you may need a slip too." I had no clue what Ms. Arnold was talking about. I was excited to get the milk and now I need to find out who this teacher was. "Ok Ms. Arnold see you later at 4:00" as I walk away back to my lunch table.

"Girl what Ms. Arnold talking to you about? Church again?" asked Rebecca. I looked at her and said, "Didn't she tell you to stay in a child's place?" We laughed and reminisced about that day. We laughed so hard I forgot to tell them about the milk. Jane said her cousin went to church before and the usher stuck her hand in her face after she got 2 good chews of gum going. "See I don't like that. Why can't I chew gum but y'all quick to give out peppermints." Jane's mom said she watches Bobby Jones Gospel every Sunday and that's when she gets a little bit of Jesus. I said *well ok*.

Chapter 3
Who Would Have Thought

The fire hydrant is on, and everyone is getting wet. School is over and its 95 degrees outside. Sometimes we play jump rope or manhunt after school. But when it's over 90 degrees with no clouds in the sky. The guys on the corner turn on the hydrant for us. The ice cream truck comes around the block too. The guys on the corner also buys everyone what ice cream we want. Daddy and mama said they are bad people and to stay away from them. They are always so nice to us, who would have thought.

We sat on my bottom step and tore that ice cream up. We had to eat it quick though, it was so hot outside the sun was melting our ice cream. "Girl when yo daddy coming home?" Serenity asked me. I shrugged my shoulders and said I don't know. See daddy has the tendency to leave for a few days at a time. Sometimes he just pops up like nothing never happened. I asked mama where do he go and she said to stay out of grown folk business.

"Well ask yo mama if you can spend the night. I'm gonna ask my momma to call yo mama and tell her I am having a little sleepover." Rebecca and Jane's mom already said yes. It's just always me. Mama and daddy are not easy people to just say yes. We agreed to all go home, change, and pack a bag. I already knew in my head what I would pack. But I can't pack anything until Serenity's mom calls my mama. We sat outside for about another 20 mins to let the sun dry us up and we all went our separate ways. The plan is in motion.

About an hour later our house phone rings. I can hear mama on the phone laughing. This is taking too long, and I actually don't even know who she is talking too. "Ok honey you take care. I will see you later, ok bye bye." The phone hangs up and I make my way to the bathroom. "Hey! You can spend the night over at Serenity's tonight. Her mother said she wants to have an end of the school year sleepover." "Oh really! Thanks mama." I packed my stuff and was out the door. Daddy and mama don't really like Serenity's mom like that. It was weird to hear her laughing on the phone. Who would have thought.

I made it to Serenity's house along with Rebecca and Jane. This isn't the first time I stayed over at Serenity's house. But it is the first time with the 4 of us. "My momma said it was easy to get your mama to say yes" Serenity told me. Sometimes we have to get Serenity's mom to help me out to get a little freedom. I am always grateful whenever she can work her magic. We all changed into our pajamas. I took a bath at home once I came inside from being wet. Mama said I smelled like outside and needed to wash my tail.

Jane pulls out this small square thing from her bag. "Oooo girl what's that?" asked Rebecca. "It's my brother beeper." "How does it work?" While Jane was schooling Rebecca on how a beeper works, I went to get something to drink. "Hey girl! How ya been?" I turned around and it was Serenity's mom. "Hi Mrs. Brownstone! I am doing great now that school is out." I laughed with her. "I know your happy cause you get a break from studying. I know yo daddy is hard on you." I took a sip and put my cup down on the counter. "Yeah, but I don't mind. The pressure isn't too bad." "Yo daddy sure has changed from back in the day."

"I didn't know y'all knew each other." "Oh yeah honey. I went to college and came back. I almost didn't recognize him. Go on in there and enjoy yourself, I'll talk to ya later." Mrs. Brownstone went into her room and closed the door. Daddy never mentioned he knew Serenity's mom from back in the day. Who would have thought.

Back in the room Jane wants to call a guy named Mike from school. She told him to page her when his parents aren't around to pick up the house phone. One time while they were on the phone his mom picked up the other phone yelling at him to hang up. Jane was so embarrassed she never called back without him giving her the green light. "Girl call yo man when you at home. It's girl time tonight. You speak to him almost every day. You so in looovveee" Serenity teased.

Truth is Serenity wanted Mike. He was going to the 9th grade, 5ft 1, smooth chocolate skin, always has the latest sneakers, his teeth were white, and his waves were on point. His smile was to die for, and he lived 4 houses down from Serenity. Jane was a stalker and found his number in the yellow pages. She called pretending to be a teacher, but he answered. He recognized her voice and immediately said "Jane it's not cool to play on people phone." She swore up and down he was so into her just because he recognized her voice. I mean how could he not she made it her business to speak to him anytime she saw him.

I think that's the real reason why Serenity told Jane she was on friend probation because who even came up with that. Serenity feels like she is prettier than Jane and dresses better. Serenity has long relaxed hair, so she always has slick ponytails. Sometimes her mom curls her ends into Shirley temple curls. She has coco brown skin with almond eyes. Jane wears clothes passed down from her older cousins. She likes to wear her hair in 2 afro puffs or just 1 big afro. Jane has dark chocolate skin and sometimes get called blacky in school. She can be insecure so Mike talking to her and giving her attention is not an opportunity she will pass up.

I hate that Jane did that to have 1 up on Serenity. They are both pretty black girls, so why be in competition. Safe to say Mike never paged her and I am glad. Serenity would have probably taken the phone and talked to him. We had pizza, did each other's nails and makeup. We played on some people phone that we didn't like. Amanda was first on list and of course she was Mike ex-girlfriend. At least Jane and Serenity could agree on something when it came to Mike. *Who would have thought.*

Chapter 4
Let The Church Say Amen

"Blessed it assurance, Jesus is mine, oh what a foretaste of glory divine. Heir of salvation, purchase of God, born of his spirit washed in his blood." Ms. Arnold and I sat 4 rows from the back at church. The people in the audience were singing. "This is my story; this is my song." I remembered to not bring any gum with me to church. Jane already warned us about what happened to her cousin. Ms. Arnold gave me a peppermint and a strawberry candy. I was happy mama and daddy changed their minds and let me come.

Ms. Arnold brought me a white dress with yellow flowers on it, white shoes with ruffles socks, and this silk skirt thing to put under my dress. Ms. Arnold said it was called a slip. Mama said it's to keep the dress from hugging your body and sticking to you. The outfit came with a pocketbook too. Mama made sure my legs were oiled up good enough. There were white gloves, but I stuffed them in my bag. I just put my sweater over my shoulders so I wouldn't be cold. "Ok you behave yourself and say a prayer for me" mama said.

I was always curious about what really happens in church.
From all the stories I've heard it started to become a little scary. But it wasn't scary at all. Everyone was so nice from the minute we walked in the church. I looked to my left and on the other side was the lady who be behind the counter

at the store. I know she not going to heaven the way she flirts with daddy and knows he's married. "Let the church say Amen" "Amen" "Let the church say Amen again" "Amen" There was a guy on the mic talking and everyone seems to be paying attention. "First giving honor to God who's the head of my life." He talked about being sick, how he prayed, and God healed him. The doctors told him he didn't have long to live but God changed that.

People were crying, clapping, and jumping up and down. The music was very loud and 2 people ran around the church. Ms. Arnold said it was a called a testimony. She said we go through tests, beat the devil, survive and tell our stories which are called testimonies. The pastor got up and preached the word. Jane said he may sound like he has asthma after every few words. To me he sounded like he was struggling to breathe. He just kept gasping for air and the mic was almost in his mouth. The guy on the organ just kept banging on the keys when the pastor talks. After he was done, they gave him a glass of water. But I think he needed a large hot tea. He will definitely have a sore throat tomorrow.

They asked people to give money for the building fund, 10% tithes, and another one for the preacher. Ms. Arnold put money in an envelope and gave me $2. We walked around in a circle and put the money in a basket. There were people in a white and gold robe singing in the choir. They sounded good too. I am going to ask mama if she knows these songs. I want to buy the cassette and play it on my radio. About 5 kids did a dance and it looked so cool. I recognized a girl from school Tatiana. Everyone called each

other Reverend, Deacon, Brother or
Sister.

Sis. Richmond walks up to me and
Ms. Arnold. "Hey Patrice! I didn't know
you had a granddaughter! She looks just
like you, especially those eyes!" "She is
one of my students at the school I work
at." "Hey pretty girl. Your dress is so
pretty." Sis. Richmond and Ms. Arnold
talked for a little bit longer before we
went downstairs to eat. I had to get me
some of the church punch everyone
always talks about. It has a little fizzle in
your throat, but it was so good. "I am

going to take you home and come back for the Ushers anniversary" Ms. Arnold said in between her sips of the church punch. "Ms. Arnold, Can I come back again next week?" I asked. "Sure! I am assuming you enjoyed yourself today." "Yes, I did. I really enjoyed the service." "Well *let the church say Amen.*"

Chapter 5
If You Only Knew

I've been going to church with Ms. Arnold for about a month now. I really enjoy it and wonder why I haven't asked to go sooner. Ms. Arnold told me mama used to sing in the choir, which I never knew that. I asked her why she didn't sing anymore and all she said was "Chile if you only knew." I made a mental note to talk to mama about that. "Girl why you so quiet today?" asked Serenity. Nothing just thinking about a few things. "Did you know your mom knew my dad back in the day?" I asked Serenity. "Yeah, she mentioned it before, but I didn't ask any further questions." "I wonder why daddy never mentioned it." Whenever he comes home, I will ask him. It's the 2nd soon so I should be seeing him.

"You see the kids across the street are finally outside?" yelled Jane. Her and Rebecca have been riding their bikes around the block. "Yeah girl let's go introduce ourselves." We walked over and said hi to the twin girls. Their names were

Whitney and Opal. They were drawing on the sidewalk with chalk. They were 8yrs old going to 2nd grade. The brother was helping his mom with bags from the car. Rebecca whispered, "Dang she must get a lot of food stamps." We all looked at her because like really, that was uncalled for. "What?!?! I'm just saying she loaded." I looked over on the mailbox and it says *"BlueBridge"*. I froze and couldn't believe it. My new neighbor is my 8th grade teacher. I give Jane a look, but she isn't catching on. The boy comes back outside but this time he is alone. "Hey what's your name?" He looks back and says, "who me?" "Yeah you, ain't nobody else around." Jane can be very sassy sometimes. "My name is Danny" he said. "Short for Daniel?" I asked. "Yeah, how you know?" he asked. "That's my daddy's name too" I said. "I was named after my father's best friend. I never met him though" he said.

Danny is 11yrs old going to the 6th grade. Both him and the twins will be going to the same school as us. Our school is from K-8th grade. We will probably all walk to school together, but his mom may drive him being that she's a teacher. Ugh I really have to do well because I do not need her coming across the street to talk to mama and daddy. "Where you from?" Rebecca asked. "Over on the east side of town. This is the first time we are moving so it's new to me" Danny said. "Oh, you from the side of town where the rich people live. So y'all don't get food stamps than" Rebecca said. "What's food stamps" Danny asked. "It's what us poor people get." "Ok Rebecca chill out, you are being rude right now" I cut her off. "Excuse Rebecca she can be a little rude sometimes." "A little?" Serenity said. If you only knew.

See Rebecca's mom don't know who her father is, at least that's what she told Rebecca. So, her mom has always struggled being a single parent. Sometimes Rebecca has these moments where she gets in her feelings when it comes to family talk. Especially a family that is doing better than her and her mom. But I told her not all 2 family households are perfect. Serenity's father sleeps around and my daddy slaps my mama around. She still not trying to hear that though. I know she is currently looking for her bio dad too. She goes to the library a lot to use their computers to do research. Her mom Ms. Sandy is always on the phone so she can't be on the computer at the same time. She has to hang up the phone in order to use the computer.

"Anyway, what made y'all move here" Rebecca asked. "My mom got a new job and dad said it was time for a change" Danny said. "What kind of change? You were getting in trouble or something?" Rebecca asked. Rebecca is nosey and always try to find a negative in someone's life or story because she feels like her life is so jacked up. She is the president of misery loves company. Maybe she needs to come to church but the building might burn down when she walks in. "I get straight A's and I was on the basketball team" Danny said. "Oh, wow something happened because who just up and moves like that?" Rebecca said. "Ok that's it, nice meeting you, see ya around" I said as I turned Rebecca around to go back across the street. "You just couldn't help yourself, could you?" I asked. "Why did you stop dead in your tracks like you seen a ghost when we were walking past the mailbox?" Serenity asked. She must have noticed when I froze like a deer in headlights after realizing my neighbor was my teacher. I looked at her and said, "If you only knew."

I was sitting in my room thinking about the events from today. I can't believe my teacher is across the street. I can tell Ms. Arnold she can stop fishing for information from other people. See I told Ms. Arnold how I was on a mission to find out who my new teacher was. She was curious too because she has been working at that school for 10 years and knows any and everybody. So, this threw her for a loop too. I have only seen her briefly throughout the summer. Maybe I can catch her one day and say hi. Spark up a conversation to see if she is mean or not.

Mama knocks on my door to tell me make sure my room is cleaned. Daddy will be home this week and expects the house to be tidy, cleaned, and dinner ready. Robbie was working on a new project trying to make a transformer. Of course, he has pieces everywhere. I help him clean up just so it is not a lot to do the day of. Robbie is mama and daddy favorite child; he basically does no wrong in their eyes. If Robbie doesn't want to eat all his vegetables he doesn't have too. He also gets privileges to drink something before he finishes his food. I am not allowed to leave the table until I finish my food and then I get something to drink.

"Hey mom can I talk to you?" I asked mama. "What is it child? I need to get this house in order before your daddy get here. And that check better be here too! I don't have time to get more makeup. That case worker needs to return my calls!" I just gave her a look because she may slap me if I say I have a guidance counselor and not case worker. I really wonder what she needs to speak to her for. I passed 7th grade, and I was #1 in my 7th grade class. I plan to be #1 for 8th grade too. "Why did you stop singing in the choir?" I asked mama. "Who lied to you and told you I sang?" "Ms. Arnold did, she said you were really good too." That lady can't keep her mouth shut mama mumbled.

The door opens and daddy walks in. "Who can't keep their mouth shut?" "Ms. Arnold told me mama used to sing really good in church" I said excitingly. "Oh, she got bored doing that, right baby" daddy said as he gave mama a kiss on the forehead. "Uh yeah I got bored and didn't wanna do it no more" mama said. "I am thinking about joining the choir too or maybe even dance." Daddy shot me a look "Over my dead body! Dance and sing your face in those books so I can get my money!" I went in my room closed my door and stuffed my face in the pillow. I cried so bad my eyes were puffy red. Why can't I sing in the choir or even dance? I get good grades so that the checks come, and they still hate me.

That following Sunday I told Ms. Arnold what happened. She chuckled and said, "Baby there is a lot of history there that you wouldn't understand." "What is there to understand" I asked very confused. As she said it out loud, I said it in my head, "Chile, *if you only knew*".

Chapter 6
Stay in a Childs Place

School starts in a few weeks. My outside privileges are basically coming to an end. I try to be outside as much as possible. I saw Daniel playing basketball across the street and went to join him. "Hey what's up, can I play?" I asked. "Yeah sure" he said. We played for about 45 mins and then his father pulled into the driveway. He got out the car and was just staring at me like he saw a ghost. For a moment I thought Danny was in trouble for playing with a girl or even worse he thought I was in their house. "Dad, dad, DAD!" Danny yelled. His father snapped out of it. This is our neighbor from across the street.

I extended my hand, "Nice to meet you Mr. BlueBridge." "Hi! Nice to meet you. Sorry I was lost in the moment you look like someone I know." "I told her earlier she has eyes like grandma" Danny said. We stopped and got ice cream while playing ball. Danny said I must see his grandma because we have the same eyes.

I asked him where she was. He mentioned his mom doesn't like when she comes around, so she stopped coming. He had no clue why, only that she keeps talking about the same thing and his mom didn't want to hear it. He said when he asks questions his mom just says, "Stay in a child's place." "Yeah, Danny is right, maybe if I can find a picture Danny can show you."

"Well, you kids finish having fun, I have some work to do. It was nice meeting you." "Nice meeting you too Mr.

BlueBridge" I waved bye. "Your dad seems pretty cool" I said. "Yeah he can be, but he is always busy on his laptop. He works at an office for a great firm. He comes home and sometimes he is still working. It's hard to get his attention and get him to do things with us. Like come outside and play ball. My mom tries to do a lot with us. Especially since she is a teacher and has the summer off" Danny said.

"It's all good, his hard work will pay off one day. That's what my parents always tell me" I said. Whitney and Opal came outside, and we were playing jump rope with them. I started teaching them how to jump double dutch being that I am the champion and all. We were drawing with chalk on the sidewalk and played hide and seek. "I wish you were our big sister Whitney said. "Yeah sometimes Danny kicks us out his room and he's mean to us" Opal followed up. I chuckled and playfully punched Danny arms. "Don't be mean to my new besties". Danny just like any other typical brother said his sisters were annoying and always bothering him. I laughed and saw my bestie coming down the block.

Serenity called me across the street. I'll catch you guys later. "See ya" I skipped across the street "Hey what's up girl" I asked Serenity. "Your dad home? Cause if not you can have dinner with us and you don't have to eat the vegetables" we both laughed as we walked to her house. I loved eating dinner with Serenity's family. Mrs. Brownstone can throw down in the kitchen. Mama sometimes doesn't cook the frozen vegetables all the way through. "What was you doing over there with the new boy?" Serenity asked. I rolled my eyes "Girl we were just playing ball, I met his dad, and played with his sisters. You weren't home earlier, and I was bored." "Look at you all meeting the family already" Serenity giggled.

"I haven't seen them yet, what's their names?" Mrs. Brownstone asked. "Their last name is BlueBridge" I said. Mrs. Brownstone dropped the dish in the sink and froze. She turned around and said are you sure. "Yeah! They have a son named Daniel like my dad and twin girls, Whitney and Opal" I said. "Oh wow, I gotta meet them" she nervously chuckled. "Mrs. BlueBridge is going to be my 8ᵗʰ grade teacher." "Is she really? Does *SHE* know you're in her class?" she asked. "No, I don't think so, I've only seen her a couple of times in passing and 1 time up close. She is new to the school and area, so I doubt she knows any of her students." I spoke.

"It was weird how Mr. BlueBridge was staring at me saying I look like someone he knew." Danny said I have his grandmother's eyes." Mrs. Brownstone mumbled under her breath, as she turned around to finish washing the dishes, I bet you do. Serenity realized her mom was acting funny. She thought this would be a good time to ask about knowing Mr. Daniel. It just seems weird Mr. Daniel barely speaks to them. He barely speaks to anyone on the block actually. Sometimes he just acts weird. Neither of his children act anything like him. Thank goodness because I don't know how we could have become friends. "I am going to go ahead home now. Thank you for dinner have a good night." I closed the door and headed home.

"Dinner was great mom" Serenity said. "Mom, Can I ask you a question?"

"Sure, what's up?" Mrs. Brownstone responded. "How do you know Mr. Daniel?" Serenity asked being very curious. "We went to school together; I went away to college and then I came back" Mrs. Brownstone answered. "Why you never talked about it?" Serenity asked. Mrs. Brownstone whipped her head around "uhhh I don't think I need to explain that to you." "Well, his daughter is my best friend. You are keeping a secret or something?" sassy Serenity asked. "I don't know who you think you're talking to, but you better stay in a child's place!" Mrs. Brownstone yelled. "I was just asking sheesh." "No, you finna get your behind whooped!" Serenity went to her room and closed the door. I see why dad have all these other women, can't even ask her a question. When I get 18, I'm out of here, I just might run away first.

All of these thoughts ran through Serenity's mind while she stretched out across her bed. She was replaying the scene she saw earlier that day. She saw Mr. Daniel arguing with Ms. Sandy, Rebecca's mom. Rebecca is at her aunt's house for the rest of the summer. School starts in a couple of weeks and Rebecca usually goes there at the end of the summer every year. She hates going there. Most of her cousins go there and she always get stuck sleeping on the couch with the plastic on it. She said her skin always get stuck to the couch and she wakes up sweaty. Her aunt's house smells like moth balls too. She said it was to keep the bugs away. So going in and out of the house was a no no. Either you're in or you're out. Can't let out her air.

Serenity is pretty good with reading lips. She saw Ms. Sandy say, "You haven't been giving me money lately." Serenity walked past and when Mr. Daniel saw her staring, she turned her head away and walked faster. Serenity is on her bed torn as to whether or not she tells her girls or keep it to herself. She wanted to tell her mom but all she will say is *"Stay in a child's place."*

Chapter 7
Now Ain't the Time

It's 2 weeks before school starts, and we are having our annual block party. The guys from the corner always rent bouncy houses, get water balloons, super soakers, pay the ice cream man to stay on the block, get all the food, and a DJ. We play in the street without worrying about cars coming. Even people who moved off the block come back for this special occasion. Mama and daddy always attend the block parties too. Sometimes it's embarrassing all the food they take back home.

One time daddy got a little box and filled it with can sodas to take back to the house. The lady from the corner store was there too. She doesn't talk to my daddy like that anymore. Ever since I've been seeing her in church. She was shoving her breast in another man's face today. Daddy didn't look so happy about it. I heard mama ask daddy what was the issue and he said now ain't the time.

There were so many people there that the street was flooded. People who didn't even live around there was showing up. I'm convinced they just wanted the free food. These girls came around with their jump rope. So, you know I ran upstairs to put on my sneakers. I came back downstairs to see Robbie playing with the super soakers. It is so good to see a smile on his face. Robbie completed 5 new projects this summer. If anyone needed a break it was him.

About 4 hours later, 3 championships later (from jumping rope), and a host of burgers and ice cream I am pooped. Whitney ran up to me saying she had to use the bathroom but couldn't find Danny. I walked her home and noticed her parents weren't home either. We went inside and immediately I can smell the incents that had been burning. Whitney ran down the hall to use the bathroom while I stayed in the living room. They had a big box color tv that sat on the floor inside of this cabinet thing. It had doors on it, and you had to open the doors to see the tv. "Very fancy" I said to myself.

The couch was a tan color with flowers on it and burgundy pillows that sat perfectly in each corner of the couch. There was a tall China glass cabinet with a dish set in there. Looks like no one ever uses that set. I always wondered why people buy dishes just to display them in a cabinet. Ms. Arnold does the same thing, makes no sense. There was an air conditioner in the living room and dining room window. I wish we had an air conditioner. I do the best I can with the box fan daddy said my checks could afford me.

They had so many family pictures hanging on the wall. You can see how everyone has changed throughout the years in all the family photos. In one photo there was an older lady who looked familiar. The twins were about 1 year old in the picture. The top part of her hair was short, the back was long, she had a bang, nose ring, and glasses. She was holding Danny while sitting in the chair. I wonder if this is his grandma, he mentioned the other day. But I only saw this lady in 2 pictures. As I was staring at the picture, I didn't even hear Whitney say she was done. I made a mental note to find out who that lady was in the picture. She looks like someone I know I thought to myself.

I turned around and said, "Did you wash your hands?" Whitney shook her head and said "mm hmm see" as she lifted both hands. As we walked down the steps to go back and join the party Danny and Mr. BlueBridge ran up to us. "Where have you been?" Danny yelled. "I had to use the bathroom and couldn't find you" Whitney whined. "Thank you for looking out for her" Mr. BlueBridge said. "You're welcome, anytime" I said with excitement.

Mr. BlueBridge stopped in his tracks like he didn't hear what I said and looked straight ahead with a serious face. I turned around and saw daddy and mama walking towards us. "I see you've met *OUR* daughter" daddy said. Mr. BlueBridge extended his hand and said, "Hi I am Neil BlueBridge, my family and I just moved around here." Daddy just looked at him and said yeah "I heard some new folks moved across the street. You know I travel a lot for work, so I am not around too much."

"Hi, I am Danny, short for Daniel" Danny said with excitement. Mama gasped and looked at daddy. "Oh really? That's my name too" daddy said while looking at Mr. BlueBridge. "Oh wow cool, I've never met another Daniel before. I was named after my dad's best friend, but I never got the chance to meet him" Danny said. Daddy looked at Danny and said "Is that right? I wonder what happened to him. Your father is a good man giving you that name." "Well, it was nice meeting you folks." Mr. BlueBridge said walking away. "Yeah you too, don't be a stranger" daddy said.

Mama turned to daddy and said, "Daniel this isn't good". Daddy put his hand up in her face walking away and said *"Now ain't the time."*

Chapter 8
Don't You Forget It

During breakfast daddy asked me if I was ready to go back to school. Of course, I wasn't but I said yes anyway. "You know what you gotta do right?" "Yes, keep getting good grades so the checks won't stop coming" I said. "Good girl". He pointed at his self and mama and said "We are your parents and have your best interest. Don't you listen to what anyone else may tell you. You hear me?" "Yes" I said. Daddy got the mail and said he was leaving for work. He kissed Robbie on the head, told him he loved him, looked at me and said, "Remember what we talked about." I nodded yes and he said, "Don't you forget it" and closed the door.

I got up from the table and went in my room. I am not allowed to go outside because school is next week. So, I look out the window and talk to my friends. Normally in the morning I just watch the birds and people on the block. I saw daddy open the car door and throw his bag in the seat. He walked over to Mr.

BlueBridge who was also at his car. He turned around and looked up at my window. I ducked down so he wouldn't see me. What could they be talking about? I thought to myself.

"Well, well, well Neil you just couldn't stay away. What the heck are you doing here?" Daniel said. "Look man, I just want to have a relationship with my daughter. I think it's time," said Mr. BlueBridge. "That wasn't the agreement! You're gonna mess up my money!" Daniel said angrily. "I've been having 2nd thoughts and want her to be a part of her real family" Neil said. "Real family?" Daniel chuckled. "I took the kid because you begged me too! I didn't have a future, couldn't go to school or play ball to advance my career! I did you and Tracy a favor!" Daniel yelled.

Neil looked at Daniel in disbelief "Kid? You took the kid? You promised to love and care for her like she was your own! You know Tracy and I couldn't go through with an abortion. Her mom was pushing for the adoption. So, we asked you as our close friend. You and your wife since you were high school sweethearts getting married anyway. That way we could see her. But you went behind our backs and made it a closed adoption and cut us completely out of her life!" "It was for the better! We found out my wife couldn't have kids and decided we didn't want y'all to change your minds. I already enlisted to go to the army. I didn't want to come home, she be gone, and seeing my wife heartbroken" Daniel explained. "But this" Daniel pointed at Neil's house "was never supposed to happen!"

"Tracy doesn't know our daughter lives across the street" Neil explained. "In fact, she doesn't know I have been keeping tabs on her all her life. I've always known where you lived, school she attended, and now she goes to church?"

"Yeah, with your crazy mother-in-law who is also the lunch lady at her school." Daniel explained. "I told Patrice not to get too close, but she couldn't help herself" Neil said. "I said no from the beginning and my wife allowed her to go. To make things worse she loves it and want to do activities in the church." Daniel said. "You coming around here with your fancy car, nice house, and perfect life! You are going

to ruin everything I have going on!”
Daniel yelled.

Neil got closer to Daniel and said “This was all a mistake, you don’t love her, and you definitely don’t treat her right. You saw what the check amount would be each month and decided to cut us off. Nothing to do with a bond. Don’t feed me that. That’s why you got that little boy ain’t it?” Daniel started walking towards his car, he turned around and said, “Stay away before I tell your wife your secrets.” Neil opened his car door and said “I know the secret you’ve been hiding for years. I can ruin you; *don't you forget it.*"

Chapter 9
This Should Be Interesting

Today is the first day of school and I am not happy. I don't like not knowing something. Is she going to be nice? Or mean? Will we get homework every night? Will she require your parents to do a meet and greet? Do we have to do projects? I have so many questions while I am walking to school with Jane. "Girl, am

I talking to myself or what?" Jane barked. "Sorry girl I really don't know what to expect from this teacher" I said. "Oh, calm down *Ms. Perfect Grades.* You act like you ever have any trouble in school. Everything just comes so easy for you. Your parents are beyond proud of you" Jane expressed. Yeah ok I said to myself.

Once we arrived at school, as always, it's a lot of people out front. There are kids who get dropped off, some kids walk, and there are even kids who walk with their siblings. Robbie doesn't go to my school. Daddy said he is too smart for this school and didn't want to waste his brains with these teachers. So, this school year Robbie goes to a special school that mama and daddy pays for. It would have been cool to walk to school with him my last year here. But I guess we can talk about our day when we get home. I stopped at the main office to get my locker number. Only 8th graders have lockers. The principal said it's to prepare us for high school. I see associates from last year in the hallway. I say hi to a few people as I am walking to my classroom #227.

I make it to the classroom and before I go in, I peek inside to see who's in the class already. There were a few knuckleheads in there sitting in the back like usual. I close my eyes, turn the knob to go in and tell myself *This should be interesting.* As always, I sit front and center to avoid getting into any trouble. Some kids are talking loud, others didn't make it yet, and no surprise to see the popular girls are gossiping. "I heard she got fired and had to come here" "Well I heard Mrs. BlueBridge isn't even her real name and she had to change it" "You can't even chew gum in her class, she will give you detention". It's so annoying to listen to them just run their mouth.

I honestly haven't really interacted with Mrs. BlueBridge. I have only spoken to her husband and children. She really just seems like a mystery. I've seen her smile in pictures only, that were in her living room. But who knows that could be a front. No one could ever find out I live across the street from her. They will 100% think I am getting special treatment. Now I am starting to panic and hope she doesn't recognize me. As always Jane interrupts my thoughts. "It's our last year here in this school and you're still choosing the front seat? C'mon and live a little bit. Come to the back with us" Jane begged. I shot Jane a look. She threw her hands up and said, "Ok suit yourself." I thought to myself maybe I should sit in the back. If I go back there maybe the teacher won't recognize me. I turned around and immediately knew I was staying right where I was. Stupid Phill was back there eating sunflower seeds, Jane was eating her lemon heads, and mind you it's around 8:30 in the morning.

The door swings open and it's the assistant principal. "Good morning class, Mrs. BlueBridge is running a few minutes behind this morning. She will be in here shortly." She turns around and leaves out the class. "OOOOO it's party time" Phill shouts out. People in the class start clapping and banging on the desks. This is Phill 3rd year in 8th grade. Yup he got left back twice. 1 year he missed too many days, last year he just wasn't doing his work. And from the looks of it he will be doing another year in 8th grade. He starts making beats with his mouth while he bangs on the desk. I guess he wants to be a rapper one day.

People crowd around him cheering him on. I can hear him saying some words, but I can't hear him clearly. Phill has always been a class clown and wanted to be the center of attention. He has an older brother named John who's locked up for robbery. He joined some gang and got caught trying to rob the corner store. John didn't even complete 8th grade and he's been locked up for 4 years now. Their dad gave up on Phill and thinks he is a loser. So, Phill has no guidance, and he is

basically raising his self. His mom left
because the dad was too abusive. He
threatened to kill her if she took the boys,
so she left them and never came back.
That was 4 years ago, and Phill never talks
about her. Word is John joined the gang
to make some money since their dad is
barely home and there was hardly any
food to eat. He had to take care of his
little brother, so he turned to the streets.

Phill said he only visited John 1 time
and he never wants to go back. I guess he
is traumatized from seeing all those scary
men in jail. They still write each other and

send pictures. I overheard daddy say their mom is a nurse now and she is doing really good. Their dad is a truck driver, and he tries to come home on the weekends. I wonder why their mom never came back after all these years. I hear people clapping so I turn around and Phill is taking a bow "Make sure y'all go buy my album when it comes out. You gotta support ya boy." I roll my eyes and turn around.

The door swings open and a lady walks in. She has on an all-black dress, green shoes that you can hear clicking on the floor, 1 bag in each hand, and she seems out of breath. Everyone scrambles to their seats. She writes her name on the board and turns around "Good morning class, I am Mrs. BlueBridge, and I will be your 8th grade teacher for this school year. To get to know each other lets introduce ourselves starting in the first row." Of course, she starts in the first row where I am sitting at, she shoots me a look and stares at me. I am praying she doesn't mention us being neighbors. It's my turn next and I don't know what to say ugh

This should be interesting.

Chapter 10
Hurry up and Tell Her

"Babe come here" Daniel yells out. "I'm coming I am getting something to drink." Sandy walks in the room and lays back down next to Daniel. "What's up" Sandy asked. "Look at this place." Daniel shows Sandy a vacation spot he saw while flipping through the magazine. "You tryna take me there or something?" Sandy sat up and shot Daniel a look. "Stop teasing me because it's not like we can be together in public. You need to hurry up and tell her." "Listen she helps take care of my kids, have some patience." "Your kids? Do I need to remind you 1 of those kids is our kid! And OUR other kid is here with me!" Sandy is fed up and tears are forming in her eyes.

"Rebecca and Robbie deserve to know the truth! I am tired of sneaking around while the kids are in school! You leave here and go back over there to her while I sleep ALONE at night!" Sandy is very emotional and starts crying. "I know babe just give me some time. I am trying to figure it all out." Daniel said holding Sandy. "What is there to figure out? Tracy and Neil are in town now. They can take their kid and we can be a family with our kids" Sandy is pleading with Daniel.

Sandy got pregnant with Rebecca a few months before Tracy got pregnant. Daniel and Sandy were messing around all throughout high school, but he left Sandy for his now wife sophomore year. But that didn't stop Sandy from seeing him. Daniel and his then girlfriend were not having sex until marriage. That was Sandy way in to keep him around. Once Daniel went to the army Sandy raised Rebecca and moved on with her life.

4 years later Sandy found out Daniel was home, and she tracked him down. They went out to talk about how he would be in Rebecca's life and one thing led to another. 9 months later Robbie was born. Daniel and his wife were having a hard time getting pregnant. He made a deal with Sandy and "adopted" Robbie as a "closed adoption". He told his wife he took care of all the paperwork, and he brought Robbie home from the hospital.

"Babe it's not that easy, she still doesn't know." Sandy stood up and wiped her face. "You mean to tell me she doesn't know her bio parents? You're over there playing house with my kid and that other kid. And she has no clue? For Christ's sake her and Rebecca are best friends! Rebecca has been going to the library trying to find her bio dad!" Sandy is now raising her voice. "I promise I will have this all fixed very soon. Baby please be patience with me." Daniel is pleading his case to Sandy. The last thing he wants is for her to tell his wife and blow everything up.

"You think giving us money around the 2nd and 3rd is enough?" Sandy said. "We need more, and my bills need to be paid on time too. You were late last month." When the check come in Daniel gives Sandy the money to take care of Rebecca. Truth is there is no check for Robbie. Sandy sends fake checks to the house "for Robbie." Daniel is the only one who checks the mail. So, his wife has no idea there is only 1 check coming in for 1 kid. Daniel wife received a large lump sum of money from her grandfather. Daniel will be writing checks from that account to "pay for Robbie's school." The checks are made out to Sandy to help her with her bills. Robbie doesn't go to a "special school" that cost money. He goes to a free charter school across town.

Daniel told his wife he took care of the paperwork for the school. Only Daniel has access to that bank account. Sandy turns around and looks at Daniel *"Hurry up and tell her!"*

Chapter 11
Must Be Nice

It's lunchtime and I can't wait to talk to Ms. Arnold. I can tell her about my new teacher, and she isn't mean after all. Today's lunch is pizza since it's the first day, school pizza is always good. Of course, the kids behind us are back at it with spoons again. Rebecca is catching us up on how Mr. Fraud is. "Yeah, he made it clear he doesn't give out homework so don't even ask" Rebecca gloated. Jane and I rolled our eyes and Jane said, "Must be nice." Although we didn't get homework today, we will have homework in the future. Mrs. BlueBridge mentioned doing projects, exams once a month, and extra credit work if possible. I kind of figured she would give out homework. I am just glad she didn't do it on the first day of school.

I am so glad she didn't mention I live across the street from her. Honestly, I don't even think she recognized me and if she did, she did a great job at pretending she didn't. During introductions of course

Phill had to "rap" his words to her. Mrs. BlueBridge was not impressed at all. She just looked at him and said that's nice and moved on to the next kid. I giggled a little bit because I don't know what Phill thought he was doing. The girls were right though, she made Jane spit her gum out. Can't chew gum in school or church sheesh.

"Let me tell y'all about ms thang in my class. Ok so y'all know Victoria right? Well, she came to school today smelling like burned up clothes, so the rumors must be true" Rebecca said. So, Victoria is a snotty cheerleader who just thinks she is the ish. She wants all the attention from the boys and thinks she is the prettiest thing around. Her father is the coach for the Bulls and her mom was a cheerleader back in the day. See where I am going with this? Must be nice. Anyway, her little brother Jason likes to mix different things. They are only a year apart. He isn't into basketball, he's more of the science type of kid. He is always trying a new experiment.

Their house caught on fire, and they have been living in a hotel. Word around the church is Jason mixed up some stuff he put together and lit a match. Once the fire started, they tried to salvage all of their "valuables" aka the expensive stuff. I am surprised Victoria would even wear any clothes from the house, especially smelling like smoke. Mama always said if you can smell yourself than someone else can smell you. So, she had to know her clothes smelled like they are burned. Victoria's mom was home when the fire broke out. She stood outside crying while the firefighters battled the flames. She was telling the firefighters to hurry up because she needed to go back and save other things.

Victoria family tried to say it was an electric fire from an old extension cord. My guess is they didn't want Jason to get in trouble or for the family to look bad. Victoria will never tell the truth because what goes on inside your house stays inside your house. You don't repeat anything that is said in your house. Parents be quick to tell you "Don't be going out there and telling everyone my business." Ever since that happened, they have been living in a really nice hotel.

Must be nice.

Chapter 12
What's That About

I got up from the lunch table to go speak to Ms. Arnold. As I am walking over there, I see her and Mrs. BlueBridge talking. Someone else would say they are arguing but knowing Ms. Arnold she could be talking about church. When she talks about the goodness of Jesus, she gets so excited and want to spread the good news. I see Mrs. BlueBridge wave her off and walk away. Maybe she is atheist or a

Jehovah Witness and don't wanna talk about Jesus. Ms. Arnold could be overwhelming sometimes. Mrs. BlueBridge looks really upset. What's that about.

10 mins before………

"How dare you come here where I work and stalk me! I haven't spoken to you in years, and you show up at my job??" Mrs. BlueBridge said in frustration. "Baby let me tell you something. I've been at this school for 10 years! TEN YEARS! Had you ever asked me how I was doing you would have known" Ms. Arnold said. "Mom, you know why I haven't been in contact with you. Who put you up to this huh? Neil, huh? Or one of those nosey "sistas" of yours at that church" Mrs. BlueBridge is on fire. "Stalking? You're one to talk when she is in your class!" Ms. Arnold shouted back. "I hope you are taking your meds because you are crazy!" Mrs. BlueBridge waved Ms. Arnold off. As she walked away, she said to herself "She's in my class?"

"Good afternoon Ms. Arnold!" I skipped over to her. Ms. Arnold wiped her face and turned around forcing a smile on her face. "There you are, I was waiting to see you. How's your day going so far?" I need to be asking you that I said to myself. "Pretty good no complaints. Mrs. BlueBridge seems ok she isn't a meanie or anything" I chuckled. "Seen a lot of new faces today?" I asked. "No not really just some here and there." Ms. Arnold lied through her teeth. "The set of twins I told you about and their brother should have started today" I reminded her. Ms. Arnold chuckled "I may have taken a break and Debbie may have seen them."

Now I don't know why Ms. Arnold is telling this lie. She likes to watch us eat the food and see our reactions. It's like when your parents sit back on Christmas watching you open the gifts, they just wrapped just to see your reaction. She has relationship with a lot of kids. Ms. Debbie doesn't really know English so Ms. Arnold kinda supervises her. So, leaving Ms. Debbie alone with the kids isn't happening. Why would she say that lie? I wonder what's that about.

"Well do you have any extra milk I can take home to Robbie?" I asked cause this was our regular thing. "Yeah I put it to the side for you" Ms. Arnold handed me a bag of chocolate milk. "Thank you so much! I saw you and Mrs. BlueBridge talking, did you 2 know each other from before?" let's see what she says. "Oh no I was telling her my testimony about my back problems. You know God has been good to me" Ms. Arnold said. That's just like Ms. Arnold to talk about God any chance she gets. But it still seemed like Mrs. BlueBridge was upset. *What's that about?*

Chapter 13
She Can't Know

Phone rings

Neil: *BlueBridge Law Firm this is Neil Speaking*

Ms. Arnold: *A nice heads up would have been nice!*

Neil: *I am sorry it slipped my mind. I'm guessing she saw you.*

Ms. Arnold: *What you think? Now she thinks I am stalking her!*

Neil: Did you tell her? She can't know. At least for right now!

Ms. Arnold: All I said was she is in your class.

Neil: WAIT! Tracy is her teacher?!

Ms. Arnold: Yes, she is. So, you need to fix this. This isn't gonna end well. She already saw us talking and asking questions.

Neil: I haven't told Tracy anything yet. I am trying to find the right time.

Ms. Arnold: The right time would have been 10 years ago when you asked me to work here and keep an eye out on her. I was good and retired doing voluntary work at my church.

Neil: Watch yourself Patrice. If you didn't make us give her up for adoption, we wouldn't be here right now.

Ms. Arnold: It's not my fault y'all thought y'all were Adam and Eve and could do what you want and get away with it! Neither one of y'all was ready to be a parent! Folks at the church were already whispering because they saw Tracy hanging with you at the mall! Y'all weren't married and was too young to be married.

Neil: There you go worrying about church folks. Let's not forget what they said about you and deacon....

Ms. Arnold: ENOUGH! I will not let you disrespect me in that manner and talk about my late husband!

Neil: *sighs* Listen I am sorry. I will figure something out and put an end to this. I want my daughter home. She isn't getting treated the way she should, and it hurts.

Ms. Arnold: Tell me about it, I can't stand Daniel. That wife of his let him do whatever he wants. He better stay away from Sandy's house before he gets caught.

Neil: That's a whole nother story for another day.

Ms. Arnold: You gotta figure something out and do it fast.

Neil: I will and please keep this between us. She can't know!

Chapter 14
Something Isn't Right

The BlueBridge family is sitting at the table eating dinner. Neil is feeling nervous because Tracy was never supposed to even work as a teacher. He makes more than enough money for her to stay home. She loves working with kids so much she still applied for a job at the school where their daughter attends. Now even worse she is in her class. She looks just like Tracy, and it is only a matter of time before she figures everything out. Tracy has been a little quiet since she has been home, something isn't right.

"How was everyone's first day today?" Neil asked in hopes Tracy will tell him about her mom and her students. "It was really good! The teachers and kids at school are pretty cool" Danny said with excitement. "Mom tomorrow can I walk to school with the kids on the block? Pplllleeeeaaasseeeee" Danny is pleading with his mom to not drive him. "Mom MOM!" Tracy snapped out of it "Yes sorry Danny." "Did you hear me?" Danny looked confused; his mom is just not herself.

"Who are these kids?" Tracy asked. "You know the girl across the street, Rebecca, Jane and Jordan; Janes brother from up the block."

"I will think about it because we are new around here and I don't know these kids" Tracy said. "Dad met them and their parents, right dad?" Neil touched Tracy shoulder massaging it "It's ok babe let him go, they are good kids. I've met them a few times over the summer." Neil does not want Tracy going to the homes to meet the parents. All hell will break lose when she makes it across the street. "Ok if dad said it's ok than I am fine with it." "We wanna go too" the twins chimed in. "Not yet you 2, you're not old enough yet." "Oh yeah mom there's a lunch lady at school who looks just like grandma" Danny said. Tracy head shot up from her plate, Neil dropped his fork.

"Are you sure it was her?" Neil asked. "Nah I'm not sure. When I walked up to get on the lunch line she walked away and went to the back" Danny said. "You know they say everyone in the world has a twin" Tracy chuckled. Neil quickly changed the subject and talked about his day and how he will work less hours at the office. Everyone was excited and finished their dinner. Neil is only cutting hours at the office to keep an eye out for everyone involved. Daniel isn't to be trusted, Tracy will probably hate him when she finds out the truth, and Patrice working at the school may not have been a good idea.

The kids have taken a bath and is in bed for the night. Kitchen is clean, food is put away, and 2 glasses of wine are waiting for Tracy and Neil. Time to address the elephant in the room. "Ok babe you wanna tell me what's bothering you?" Neil asked Tracy. Tracy looks at Neil and says, "You wouldn't believe me if I told you Danny was right about who he saw at lunch today." Neil looks confused or least he's trying to. "Yeah, I know the look on your face says it all. That's how I felt when I saw her. I mean, can you believe it? After all these years she pops up out of nowhere. She claims she has been working there for 10 years!" Neil says "Well if she has been there for 10 years than she isn't just popping up. It's not like she is stalking you. What was her reaction to seeing you?"

Tracy is confused as to why Neil isn't equally upset with her. Patrice made them gave their first child up for adoption, the whole church turned against them, and she threw it in Tracy face every chance she got. Anytime she would come around she started asking Tracy if she knew where her other child was, and it was about time she be a *mother* to all of her kids. Tracy could care less how long Patrice been working there. She doesn't wanna be around her mother at all! But on the flip side Neil seems like he is giving Patrice a pass or some grace. Tracy thought to herself *something isn't right*.

Chapter 15
Wait What You Mean

Danny has been walking to and from school with us for the past 2 weeks. He's cool to be around and to my surprise daddy hasn't said a word about him walking with us. Maybe it's because they have the same name; but oh well who knows. "So how y'all liking y'alls teachers?" Danny said. Jane waved her hand "Boy please yo momma our teacher and you think we are gonna tell you the truth?" I laughed and said true dat, you might go back and snitch. Truth is I don't think he will, but I am still trying to figure Mrs. BlueBridge out. It is kinda hard to read her some days. I know I gave her the side eye when she gave us a 5-page essay to do! Like c'mon school just started, and she is giving out essays. "I am preparing you for college" Mrs. BlueBridge shouted. "What if some of us don't wanna go to college" Phill yelled. Needless to say, the class was not happy about it.

"What about your teacher Danny?" I asked. "He is cool, we don't get homework on Fridays which is great because I could relax. Oh yeah, I forgot to tell y'all I think I saw my grandmother working as a lunch lady on the first day. But for some reason every time I go to lunch, I don't see the lady anymore" Danny explained. "It's only 2 lunch ladies, Ms. Debbie and Ms. Arnold. And I know Ms. Debbie isn't your grandmother, she doesn't really know English" Jade said. I chimed in "Plus Ms. Arnold never mentioned anything about having any grandkids. Are you sure you saw her? You said before it's been years since you saw her. She probably doesn't even look the same." Danny chuckled and said, "Yeah you're probably right." "How don't you know what your grandmother looks like?" Jane asked. "It's been years since I have seen her. She used to be around all the time and then one day it just stopped" Danny said.

"Your mom never said why?" Jane continuing to be nosey. "Nah she doesn't like talking about it" Danny answered. "Hmm you got a deadbeat grandma like I got a deadbeat dad. Here today gone tomorrow" Jane said. "Wait what you mean" Danny asked looking confused

"JANE!" I yelled. "That was rude!" "Look I'm just saying, it's a reason why his grandmother stopped coming around. Something must have happened" Jane said. I had to cut Jane off from talking. She started to act like Rebecca because she is the one who could care less what comes out of her mouth. I would tell him to sneak into our lunch period by just getting a bathroom hall pass but he can get caught. I don't wanna put him in that situation for a look alike. I know Ms. Arnold doesn't have any grandkids, there's absolutely no pics of anyone in her house besides herself. I would be surprised if she mentions she has any family at all.

I wish I knew my grandparents. Mama, daddy and Robbie are the only family members I know. I never met any aunts, uncles, cousins, or anyone else that doesn't live in my house. Daddy said him and mama moved from their home state to where we are now, and we don't have the money to go visit anyone. Don't ask me to ever create a family tree, it will be incomplete. I'm gonna tell Rebecca to let Danny go with her to the library. Rebecca still goes to see if she can find her father.

Maybe Danny will be able to locate his grandmother. "Y'all going to Rebecca's birthday party next month?" Jane asked and snapped me out my zone as always. "Yeah, I heard she was making it a Halloween party" I said.

I gotta ask mama if she can take me to the salvation army to get a costume. It's before the 2nd so that means the check won't be here in enough time for me to get something new. That's if we can even afford it. I like to dress up for Halloween and go trick or treating. This year I really don't want to poke holes in my sheet to be a ghost. Serenity's mom brought my costume last year. Serenity and I dressed alike as Phil and Lil from Rugrats. "Do you know what costume you might get?" I asked Jane. "I was thinking about being Sailor Moon."

"You should be Darla and Danny should be Alfalfa" I said laughing while entering school. "He will never be my love interest" Jane said as she walked away. Danny stood there and replayed the conversation before looking up saying *"Wait what you mean"*.

Chapter 16
You Oughta Be Grateful

We are all sitting at the dinner table eating mamas delicious Sunday dinner. She made baked chicken, white rice, black eye peas, baked macaroni and cheese, string beans, and corn bread. She said we can bake a cake later. She normally makes collard green with neckbones, but she chose string beans instead. Oh yeah can't forget the fruit punch Kool-aid. Lately I noticed mama has been in a better mood until daddy comes around. It's like she doesn't want to show him she's smiling or that she is even happy.

"Church was great today! Do you wanna know what the preacher talked about?" I spoke. "Nope we don't want to hear it. Is it bringing any money in my house? I didn't think so. You need to make sure those grades stay the way they are. I don't even know why you wanna go every week. I should have said no. You oughta be grateful!" daddy yelled. I looked at mama for a little help but as always, her head was down. She never has my back when daddy tells me no or just yells at me for no reason. I know for sure now we aren't baking that cake. I sat at the table while I listened to daddy talk to Robbie about his teachers and the kids at his school.

I am glad Robbie loves his new school. One of my fears was that he would feel afraid and alone in a new school. I can't wait to see what projects he comes up with. "Can we go get costumes for Rebecca's Halloween birthday party?" I asked hoping daddy would say yes. "That little bit of money you get isn't enough for a Halloween costume. I can get Robbie a costume because he always has money left over." Daddy said while throwing away his food. Daddy placed his hand on Robbie's shoulder and said "Plus son there are some people at the party you can meet. It will be good for you." What is daddy even talking about? Everyone knows Robbie is not the social type. He would let me use his leftover money for a costume because I know he doesn't wanna go or even care to go. "So, what am I going to wear to the party?" I asked holding back tears.

"You and yo mama can figure it out, y'all always do. I better not see a tear drop!" daddy said as he walked away. I wiped the tears from my face when daddy wasn't looking. I always wish every year that I would be able to get a new Halloween costume. I know a lot of kids will be Power Rangers this year. I wanted to be the pink Power Ranger and tell Serenity to be the yellow Power Ranger. Last year some kids were Barney, Ninja Turtles, and even Catwoman. I am going to see what Serenity is wearing, maybe her mom will buy me a costume this year if Serenity and I come up with a theme. Hopefully the stupid kids from 2 blocks over don't throw any eggs on Halloween.

They were stupid high school kids, and they went around throwing eggs at people car windows and then wrapping it in tissue. Some people stopped giving out candy to not deal with those kids. Sucks for us because we knew which houses to go to, to get the good stuff. They would give out king size candy bars and sometimes even money. The bell rings and I stopped day dreamer. Mama answered the buzzer, and it was Serenity. I went downstairs to talk to her. "Hey girl, what you were up too?" Serenity asked. "Nothing just got done eating dinner." I spoke. "What are you wearing to Rebecca's party? I was just talking to my mom about costumes. Your dad acting cheap again?" Serenity asked.

See this is why Serenity is my best friend. She knows how my family is well daddy mainly. She always looks out for me, daddy said it's because she feels sorry for me. But I know that's not true.

"You must have been reading my mind cause I just asked mama and daddy for a costume." "Oooooh girl you know I'm a mind reader" we both laughed. "So, I was thinking we would dress up as Gina and Pam from Martin" Serenity said.
I looked at her like she was crazy. "Now you know mama and daddy will not let me dress like them. Obviously, I would be Pam and she do be having fly outfits just not for kids to dress up as" I said. "Girl you could change your clothes when you get to Rebecca's party." "Nice try, mama and daddy are both going to the party."

Serenity looked surprised and said, "Your daddy is actually coming to an event with y'all?" "I know right, he's always gone, and he also told Robbie there is some people he could meet" I said. Serenity was stuck in another zone, and I called her name at least 4x before she snapped out of it. "I wonder if that's what him and Rebecca's mom was talking about. I saw them talking back in the summer before school started. She looked like she was going off on him, but I kept it moving" Serenity finally admitted. Why would daddy be speaking to Ms. Sandy? And she was going off on him? He probably was being rude and disrespectful. Ms. Sandy seems like the type to not take no mess from anyone. "Hmmm maybe we will find out at the party. I have no clue who Robbie needs to meet. If introvert was a person Robbie, is it" we laughed.

We caught up about school and how Serenity's dad took the new secretary out for lunch, so we know what that means. Serenity says "I told my dad it's embarrassing because of the rumors. I wish he would just stop and just love my mom. He said that ship has sailed and not many kids can go to the schools I have been too. He looked at me and said You oughta be grateful".

Chapter 17
Did She Just Say That

Mrs. BlueBridge has a video playing in the class and of course we will have to write a report on it. The video is about The American Revolution. I have read about it thanks to daddy buying me books so I can constantly study, so I kind of zone out and start daydreaming. Serenity and I never finalized our costumes for Rebecca's party. I am going to stick with the pink and yellow Power Rangers. I would love to dress up as Pam and Gina, but I know daddy wouldn't go for it. He isn't open minded to see the fun in things. But I can't believe Serenity told me about daddy and Ms. Sandy. It's very weird because daddy literally doesn't bother with anyone on the block. I ran out of ideas as to why they would be arguing. I know Serenity wouldn't make that up. Daddy had to be rude or disrespectful.

"Ok class a 3-page report is due next week" Mrs. BlueBridge announced. We can never catch a break; I think I've written 5 papers already since school has started. I'm going to ask if I can go to the library with Rebecca and study. Maybe I will tell Daniel to come too so he can find his grandmother and put this whole lunch lady thing to rest. I don't know why he just can't ask his mom since she works here. It's not like she will lie to him. That's it, I'm gonna tell him to ask his mom, there problem solved. "Ahhh we can't never watch a movie and not have to do a report?" Phill complained. He is saying what we all are thinking. Mrs. BlueBridge walked away like she didn't hear him and opened her grade book. "Phill from the look of your grades. You should be asking for extra credit" Mrs. BlueBridge outted Phill. The whole class laughed, and Phill just slid down in his seat quiet as a mouse now.

Mrs. BlueBridge handed out some papers to everyone. Mine had a note attached to it.

You are excluded from the 3-page paper

I am surprised she excluded me from this assignment. Do I dare ask her why? Do I keep this to myself? Am I the only one who got a pass? I gotta hide this note and don't let anyone see it. When Mrs. BlueBridge gets back to her desk, she doesn't even look at me. I don't want to make it awkward, so I play it cool. It's bad enough she lives across the street from me, I don't need anyone to think I am getting special treatment. I will still go to the library and tell Rebecca to invite Serenity. That way we can figure out our costumes. I will still do research (just not as much) so no one will become suspicious. On the way home I will tell Rebecca and Danny. Class is over and it's time to go home. I wrote a note and

passed it to Mrs. BlueBridge on my way
out the classroom.

Thank you so much. I appreciate you ☺

Danny, Rebecca, Jane, and I walk
home together every day after school. I
told them the idea I had about going to
the library. Of course, I didn't mention my
studying would be fake. We agreed to go
to the library tomorrow straight after
school. That way I can ask mama and
daddy tonight if I can go. Of course,
everyone else parents will automatically
say yes. Hopefully mama and daddy say
yes with no problems, since "it is for a

project." "Rebecca since you know the programs to search for your dad. Maybe we can search for my grandmother" Danny said. "Why don't you just ask your mom and tell her what you saw?" Jane asked. My thoughts exactly. Danny explained to us he told his parents at dinner he thought he saw his grandmother, but his mom said it wasn't her. So now he wants to find is grandmother.

Mama and daddy said I can go to the library. Daddy said he wanna see all the notes and information I find while being at the library. I would have to be quick because I really need to speak with Serenity. I laid across my bed and turned the tv to watch The Magic School Bus. I wish I had a teacher like Mrs. Frizzle. All the adventures and trips the kids go on would be so much fun. Maybe we could go take a trip inside daddy brain and see why he is always so mean. I giggled to myself and got up to go get a glass of water. Nothing new I hear daddy and mama in the room arguing.

I tiptoe to the kitchen to get something to drink, and I didn't even have to do that. They are so loud they didn't even hear me, but I can hear them. "You are always treating her like a kid on the street. You never do that to Robbie. You really need to stop!" "Well, she basically is ain't she? I did them a favor and you know that! A deal is a deal!" "Wow nice to know how you really feel! You act like Robbie is so much different than her! They are equally the same!" "See that is where you are mistaken! Because they are not!" "Dan what the hell you mean they aren't? We adopted them both! The only difference is, we know who her biological parents are but not

Robbie's!" I dropped my glass on the

floor. Did she just say that?

Chapter 18
I Need Answers

"Girl, you don't hear me calling you?" Serenity asked me while I snapped out my thoughts. "I'm sorry girl, I was zoned out." "Yeah, that's like the 5th time already since we been here" Serenity said. "You good? This is not like you at all. You seem so lost." I told her I was fine even though I wasn't. After I heard what mama said I ran back in my room and stared up at the ceiling basically all night. I was trying to make sense of what she said. I kept replaying it in my head over and over ***"We adopted them both! The only difference is, we know who her biological parents are but not Robbie's!"*** I haven't told Serenity or anyone else. I am so lost and played different reasons over in my head as to why she would say that. Maybe she meant they adapted to the feel of loving us or they adapted to being parents with 2 kids.

If that's what she meant than I get it because it's not easy raising 2 kids. On top of making sure they have good grades, making you look good, and not embarrassing you. But what really doesn't make sense is when she said they knew who my biological parents were but not Robbie. Biological means mama didn't give birth to me. If she didn't, then who did? Poor Robbie he has absolutely no clue. I don't know if I should even tell him, tell mama I heard them, or tell daddy I heard them. I am afraid I will get punished and be told to stay in a child's place. I really need someone to talk too. The only other adult I trust is Serenity's mom Mrs. Brownstone.

Serenity interrupts my thoughts again, "So we are going to be the pink and yellow rangers? I will tell my mom to pick up our costumes." "That sounds good to me" I responded. I don't even want to go to the party anymore. I got up and went to the computer with Rebecca and Danny to see what progress they've made. "So, I went through my mom's stuff to find my grandma's maiden name. I found Patrice Concord." Danny shared. "Isn't Mrs. Arnold first name Patrice?" Rebecca asked. "Why y'all looking at me?" I asked. "Well, you go to church with her every Sunday, don't tell me you don't know her first name" Serenity said. "Yeah, it's Patrice, but her last name is Arnold not Concord." "Well, that excludes her, unless she got married" Rebecca said. "Nah she wasn't married to my knowledge" Danny said.

"Well, you need to find out if she ever got married. We can parking lot Mrs. Arnold for now. Online doesn't say anything about this Concord lady y'all found being married?" Serenity asked. "Yeah, it says her husband died in 1980. But there is no name" Rebecca said. "What website is this because it seems like the information isn't legit" Serenity said. "This is a creditable website; I use it all the time." Rebecca barked back. I know Rebecca feels some type of way towards Serenity. Since we've been at the library Serenity has been acting bossy. Like she is rushing them or think they are wasting their time with the research they are doing. "Look I will ask my mom and dad about my grandmother being married. I wrote down a lot of this information to take back home with me" Danny said.

Rebecca found her mom's yearbook and wondered if her mom dated anyone in the yearbook. I looked through the yearbook and saw mama and daddy. I had to stop looking once I realized I didn't have any notes for the paper. Daddy reminded me before I left the house to make sure I came here to study and not meet up with boys. I don't know where he would get that from. I hang out with all girls and don't even have male friends besides Danny. I thought I heard Danny say his mom and dad was in the yearbook too, but I quickly dismissed it as I was searching for a particular book. Even though I had notes already down in my book. I wanted to add new information to make my notes look really good.

I was able to create 3 pages of notes as a draft for my paper. I ended up just writing the entire paper since I was already in the groove. Rebecca's party is next week, and I need to get out of this funk I am in. But I don't know if I can. Maybe I will do what Danny and Rebecca are doing. I don't know where I would start but all I know is that I need answers.

Chapter 19
Oh You Didn't Know

For the past week daddy has been home less and less since that blow up he and mama had. I saw him taking things out the house like clothes and I think he has been staying at a hotel. Mama hasn't been too sad lately, but I heard her asking daddy where he's been. The first is in 2 days which is Sunday so the checks may come today. "We need groceries and I need to feed the kids." Mama pleaded. "I will take care of it, pretty soon it will be 1 kid you need to worry about." Daddy said as he slammed the door and left. "Mama is daddy leaving us?" I asked. "He will if your check doesn't come!" mama walked away and slammed her door.

I reached over and grabbed Robbie's hand at the table. "It's going to be ok." He pulled back and finished his breakfast. He got up from the table and went into his room. My stomach is in knots, and I do not have an appetite. I feel like my whole world is crashing and somehow, it's my fault. If I didn't be such a brat and ask for the costume, just gotta learn to be grateful for what mama and daddy could afford. Mama and daddy wouldn't have gotten into the fight, and we would all be at the table eating breakfast together. Robbie hasn't said a word all morning and I feel like I let him down. I try to protect him, get all the punishments, get all the bad treatment, and basically get all the 2nd hand treatment. Life was going great well at least for Robbie 90% of the time. I think I just messed that up.

Today we have a half day because of the Halloween parade at school. A lot of kids came dressed up with their costume on. I left mine home because tomorrow is Rebecca's party and I know everyone will have a different costume just for the party. I was fortunate enough to get 1 decent costume, so I won't waste it on a half day at school. "Why didn't you wear your costume?" Jane asked. "I woke up late and was rushing so I will save it for the party tomorrow. Now I don't need another costume for the party." I lied through my teeth. Only Serenity knows the truth about my home life. I don't share it with others.

I am going to ask mama if I can stay at Serenity house tonight. Hopefully she says yes and that gives me a chance to talk to Mrs. Brownstone. Maybe me being away will be best for everyone at the moment. I know she can't stomach looking at me. Especially if the checks don't come and daddy is in a bad mood. At that point she will definitely say no. I can stay with Serenity all day and go to the party from her house. I will just go home after the party. Fingers crossed Mrs. Brownstone can give me some answers. Being that she went to school with daddy and have known him for

years. I know she won't lie to me. I know I
will not be ok until I have the answers I
need.

It's time to go to gym class and Jane
ran up to me out of breath. "Dang girl
slow down let me catch up." Jane said. I
stopped and let her catch her breath even
though I didn't want to. I really just want
to be left alone. I am in no mood to speak
with anyone. If I can lock myself in my
room and put a pillow over my head, I
would. We stopped near the cafeteria and
saw Danny talking to Mrs. Arnold. He past
her a piece of paper and Mrs. Arnold gave

him the biggest hug. Danny didn't walk to school with us this morning, so I had no idea he was going to even talk to Mrs. Arnold. "Wow he really did it." Jane said. I looked at her and said, "Did what?". "You haven't heard?" Jane asked.

Jane explained Danny asked his parents about Patrice Concord. Mrs. BlueBridge came out and told the truth that Patrice Concord was his grandmother. She left the part out that her married name was Arnold. Danny told Jane it seemed like his mom was hiding something and his dad barely said a word.

Until his mom left out to run an errand and his dad spilled the beans. Arnold was her married name and her husband died in 1980. Danny said when he saw Mrs. Arnold, he would give her his information. He has a lot of questions that are not answered. "I don't know what I would do if my parents lied to me about my family. I mean his grandmother worked in the school he attends, and his mom works at. Why would Mrs. BlueBridge not tell the truth?" Jane said. I just looked at Jane in disbelief. Jane looked at me and said, "Oh you didn't know."

Chapter 20
This Has to Be a Dream

I don't know who my birth parents are (if that is even true), Robbie possibly has different parents as well, and now Mrs. Arnold is Danny grandmother. This is why you gotta stop snooping for stuff because you may not like what you find. I have yet to talk to Danny to find out how he is doing. I still haven't told anyone about the drama in my house. Daddy is here and of course mama said no to staying with Serenity tonight. Daddy has been in Robbie's room buttering him up. I heard them laughing a few times too.

When I go to church Sunday, I am actually gonna go to the altar for prayer. My mind and thoughts are not in a good place. I am starting to have built up anger. Because everything leads to why. Mrs. Arnold has a lot of explaining to do. Because she never mentioned having kids and she knew who Danny was. Maybe he was right, and she ran to the back when she saw him. Makes sense as to why she was arguing with Mrs. BlueBridge. But again, everything leads to why. My door swings open and it's daddy. "I heard you asked your mama to go over to Serenity house tonight and she said no. I also don't want you going to church with that lunch lady anymore either. Nothing good is going to come from that" he walked out and closed my door.

Could it get any worse? I can feel the walls closing in on me. I looked out the window as the kids were playing outside before the streetlights came on. I saw Serenity, wrote notes on a piece of paper and stuck it to the window like a sign so we can communicate. The signs read We need to talk, I hate my life, Don't ring the bell they will say no, I will see you at the party tomorrow. I ripped the papers up into little pieces and stuffed them under my bed. I will get rid of them little by little. She gave me a thumbs up and went on home. I saw Danny outside with his sisters and Mrs. BlueBridge was on her porch reading a book. Danny seems to be laughing like everything was ok. That's good for them, I guess.

I laid down on my bed trying to force myself to sleep. I don't want to eat dinner, I just want to close my eyes, wake up and I am 21. I will be an adult and on my own. I will have a house, husband, and children. If all men are like daddy and Serenity's father than I will be alone and just live my life. I will check in on Robbie and spoil his kids whenever he has some. I will basically be the rich auntie with color TVs in every room. I don't need to beat the streetlights; I can come home when I want too. I will be able to eat whatever I want and if I don't want vegetables, I simply just won't eat them.

No one will be able to tell me what to do. I only have 9 more years until I am free.

Everyone is having fun at Rebecca's party. A little bit of everything was there from, Barney, to Ninja Turtles, to Woody and Buzz Lightyear. Just like I predicted no one had on their costume from yesterday. Serenity and I are killing it with our Power Ranger costumes. We will have to wait a week before we can see the pictures. Her mom has to turn the film in so the pictures can be printed. Sometimes she gives them the entire camera to have the pictures printed. I like how the pictures come out on the disposal camera better and to my luck she has a disposal camera tonight. We always laugh when we get the pictures back because sometimes, we get people heads, or the side of their face, or we miss the person completely. We never know how they look until we pick them up.

I noticed daddy and Ms. Sandy talking a lot and mama was talking to Mrs. Brownstone. Even Jane asked me why my daddy and Ms. Sandy was so cozy all of a sudden. Serenity gave me a look and I turned my head away. Daddy walked over to Robbie and walked him back to Ms. Sandy. After about 2 minutes Ms. Sandy went and got Rebecca and brought her over to their corner where they were talking. Right now, I am just confused so I walk over to mama and ask her what was going on. She waved me off and told me I caused enough trouble and to finish having fun before my night ends early. I turned around to walk away and heard Mrs. Brownstone say, "Umm honey why is Sandy rubbing her hand up and down Daniels arm?" Mama walked over to them, there was some yelling, mama grabbed Robbie's arm and daddy grabbed him back, and next thing you know Ms. Sandy face is in the punch bowl.

Rebecca ran away crying and Jane went after her, Mrs. Brownstone grabbed mama and brought her outside. Everyone is looking at me and I can feel the walls closing in again just like last night. Jane walked back in the room, came over to me and said "You knew? She went to the library almost every day looking for her dad and she is your sister!" I am stuck frozen in place, while I see Janes mouth moving, I can't hear any words that are coming out. **She is your sister** is echoing in my mind. I see Serenity jump in Jane's face, but I have no clue why. It is pure chaos for a good 5 minutes before I came back down to planet earth. "Jane what are you even talking about?" I shouted. "Don't act like you care and stop playing dumb!" Jane yelled at me. "Yo chill out Jane! She didn't know!" Serenity barked at Jane. "Well, your father introduced Robbie to Ms. Sandy and told him that's his real mom. Ms. Sandy told Rebecca your dad is her real father." Jane explained.

Jane explained how it all went down. Ms. Sandy came up to dad and said it was now the secret comes out or she will blast it in front of everyone all by herself. Once Robbie and Rebecca were around, daddy explained who was who and proceeded to say he was moving in so they can all be a family. Mama walked over asking what was going on and Ms. Sandy said, "I finally got my man back." Ms. Sandy told mama the truth about Rebecca and Robbie than daddy followed up with he was leaving her to be with his family. Mama asked them to repeat themselves and before Ms. Sandy got 2 words out mama had her head in the punch bowl. I told Jane I didn't know and also confessed what happened in my house within the past week.

Rebecca walked over to us with puffy red eyes. At this point the lights are on, and the party is over. "Hey sis" Rebecca said very sarcastically. I closed my eyes and say to myself, this has to be a dream.

Chapter 21
Is That Daniel

After the party the next day, daddy and mama was arguing so I left without them even noticing. I went and sat on the porch because he started slapping her around. Mama wanted answers and daddy wouldn't give them to her. She was angry and confused just like we all were. He seemed like he didn't care, the more she cried the angrier he got. Robbie is at Ms. Sandy house, so I was there alone. I was angry because I feel like Rebecca stole my family. Daddy and Robbie are now gone, and mama wouldn't even talk to me when we got home.

I cried asking questions and before she closed the door in my face, she looked at me and said, "You're next." The next morning was so quiet, and Robbie's room was already empty. Who? How? And when? I didn't hear anyone come in here and I didn't hear any noise. I knocked on mama's door and of course she didn't answer. I went to the kitchen to make some cereal and the milk was expired. I just ate dry cereal in hopes mama comes out the room soon and go get milk. I hear a key in the door, and it swings open, daddy is here. He looks at me and says where your mama at and I point to the room. Before I could even ask him to get milk, he was already in the room closing the door.

I hear them yelling, screaming, and crying, well mama was crying. I heard daddy say "This what you wanted; I didn't want this. Things happened, one thing led to another and now Sandy and I have 2 kids together." Things were being thrown so I got dressed and went outside on the porch. It's still pretty early and there are people already outside walking, jogging, or just simply sitting on their porches. Mrs. BlueBridge came out her house, waved and said good morning before she got in her car and left. Danny came out the house and ran across the street after Mrs. BlueBridge pulled off. "Hey, how are you? I know yesterday was a lot and a total disaster." I told him how mama and daddy were upstairs arguing now that's why I am outside.

Danny asked me what I was going to do. I gave him a look because look at me, outside on the porch in pajamas, parents upstairs fighting, and to add salt to injury they don't even like me. What is there for me to do? Mama won't even talk to me and blames all of this on me. What really hurts is she said I am next. Will she send me off to another family? Is it true she isn't my birth mom (I mean it's true for Robbie) and she will send me with her? I have so many questions. I told Danny I will try to talk to mama again and see what happens. I doubt I get anywhere.

"Well let's talk about you for a little bit. I heard your dad came clean and Mrs. Arnold is your grandmother." Danny put his head down and said, "Yeah about that, it's been rough." I was shocked he said rough. I thought it would be 1 big family reunion, but I was wrong.

Danny explained his mom exploded when she found out his dad told the truth. His parents haven't been speaking and his dad has been sleeping on the couch. His mom won't explain why she doesn't want Danny to have any contact with his grandmother. He sneaks to speak with her at lunch time since our grade goes after his grade. He pulled a picture out of his pocket. "Remember I told you;

you look like someone I know? Look that's my grandma, you have the same eyes as her." I was staring at a picture of Mrs. Arnold, but it didn't look like Mrs. Arnold. The lady I saw in the picture had straight black long hair, crop top, jean shorts, and LA Gear sneakers on with high socks. I didn't see the resemblance, but I kept it to myself. Danny found a box of stuff in the attic and has been going through it little by little. He waits until his parents aren't home and look at the pictures that are in there and it's mostly pictures of Mrs. Arnold. He hasn't gone through the paperwork yet, but he will read it one day.

Mrs. BlueBridge pulled up in her car and Mr. BlueBridge was coming out of the house. Danny hurries up and stuffed the picture back in his pocket. "I gotta do my chores I'll catch you later" Danny said as he ran back across the street. He helped his mom with the bags from the car. Mr. BlueBridge waved hello and gave Mrs. BlueBridge a kiss on the cheek. "I feel so bad for her, everything she knows to be her life is a lie" Mr. BlueBridge said. "Yeah, poor thing. I could tell you 1 thing. Her grades haven't slipped at all. She is so smart and driven" Mrs. BlueBridge said. Daddy came out the door and saw me sitting on the steps. "You can go on upstairs now. Don't call me for anything there's no need too. I will stop by to check the mail until my address change goes through. It can take a couple of years."

Mrs. BlueBridge was still on her porch and saw the interaction across the street. She didn't get a chance to meet all her students' parents, so she wanted to see his face. Daniel walked to his car to throw his things in the back seat. Mrs. BlueBridge turns around asked her husband in disbelief "IS THAT DANIEL?"

Chapter 22
I Just Wanna Know Why

It's been a week since the truth came out, Serenity, Jane, Rebecca, and me all sit in Serenity's living room to try to make sense of life at the moment. Rebecca said it is weird having Robbie and daddy at the house. She still can't believe all that has been happening in the past week. Daddy has been telling her what to do like he has been there all her life. Ms.

Sandy told her to get used to them being a family. Robbie doesn't speak to anyone, barely even daddy. I miss Robbie so much. I know he doesn't like change, so I know he is going through a rough time right now. I've been at Serenity's house more often after school. I spent the night yesterday and it seems like mama don't care what I do.

She is always in her room with the door closed. I eat dinner at Serenity's house every night before I go home because mama doesn't cook. All the food in the fridge went bad and mama said she will get groceries but hasn't yet. I leave earlier to go to school so I can eat breakfast, I eat school lunch and dinner at Serenity's house. Rebecca takes the milk for Robbie because I told her he likes them. Maybe that will help their relationship. But knowing Robbie it will take a little while longer. The first day back to school after all the drama was the worst. Everyone was at the party, so you know I wanted to go to school with a bag over my head. I wanted to stay home but mama said no of course. Questions were coming from everywhere, "So is Rebecca your sister?" "Your dad cheated on your mom?" "Who does your dad live with now?" "Did you not know?"

I wish Serenity was here to be my security guard, tell these kids to back up, and leave me alone. I ate lunch in the classroom with Mrs. BlueBridge for 3 days straight, to get away from the kids in the cafeteria. "How is your mom doing?" Mrs. BlueBridge asked. "She doesn't talk to me. All she does is stay in her room. I heard her crying yesterday but when I knocked, she didn't answer the door." Mrs. BlueBridge heart just sank in her stomach. To say she felt bad for her student was an understatement. She also couldn't shake off the feelings that she saw Daniel. Daniel the same man that adopted her daughter she had to give up. She made a mental note to talk to Neil about it. "If you need anything you can always come talk to me. If you need to eat lunch in here for the rest of the school year you can do that as well." Mrs. BlueBridge said with a smile. It felt good to have someone who genuinely cares. The only other adult that cared for me is Mrs. Brownstone. We laughed and played games for those 3 days I was in the classroom. I really liked Mrs. BlueBridge and Danny was lucky to have her as a mom. I don't understand why Mrs. Arnold was kept a secret from him.

Speaking of Mrs. Arnold, I saw her my first day back eating in the cafeteria. "How ya been baby?" Mrs. Arnold asked. "Not good, not good at all." "You know you can come back to church with me on Sundays." I gave her a look and said "Now you know everybody in there knows what happened. That's the last place I wanna be. All church people do is gossip." Mrs. Arnold shook her head and said "You can go to the altar for prayer. No one needs to know what you are praying about." "I don't know, I will think about it. It hurts knowing your family member kept a secret from you all of these years. Everything and everyone I knew to be family is 1 big lie." Mrs. Arnold just wanted to grab her grandbaby and tell her everything will be ok, but she knew she would make things worse.

I looked at Mrs. Arnold and said "I know you can relate. Danny told us what happened." Mrs. Arnold looked at me and said "Excuse me? Now you watch your mouth young lady." "Danny was lied to just like I was, and you were 1 of the people keeping the secret. At least for him everyone doesn't know. I don't understand why you adults are all lying."

"No one is telling a fib" Mrs. Arnold barked back. "Now you mind your manners. I know you're hurt but you are still a child." I looked at Mrs. Arnold and said, "I just wanna know why."

Chapter 23
So What Are You Tryna Say

Neil checks his voicemails and notices he has 1 from Tracy. "Hey babe, hope you're having a great day. Don't make any plans to work while you are home tonight. There is something I need to discuss with you. Talk to you later love you". Neil puts the phone down and immediately he knows Tracy is going to ask about Daniel. He is nervous to tell his wife that their little girl is in her class, he has been keeping track of her with the help of her mother, and most of all he wants her home with them. Maybe with Daniels secret coming out she will be on the same page with bringing their little girl home. It pains him to see his daughter being neglected. He is ready to come clean and tell Tracy everything.

Neil turns to his client and says "Ok so I will get all of this to the courts and have him served. It may take a while but trust me it will get done." "Thank you so much. He thinks this is over, but it is far from over. I will have the last laugh" the lady stated. "Ok let me walk you to the door. Remember if you need anything please let me know. Do not contact him or let him know what's coming. We don't want him trying to get ahead of this." The client put the envelope in her bag. Neil closed the door and started gathering his belongings to get ready to go home. He helps people every day win their cases and he isn't sure if he can help himself. Thanksgiving and Christmas is right around the corner, and he would love for his family to be together including his little girl. The twins already love her, and she is like Danny's female best friend.

Neil pulls into his driveway and takes a deep breath before he goes into the house. Dinner is ready but that wasn't out of the norm. Tracy greeted him with a kiss and the kids were running around, nothing was out of the norm. Neil put his briefcase down on the floor, keys on the table, and sat down next to Danny on the couch. He proceeded to ask Danny how school was, if he had homework, and most of all has he spoken to his grandmother. Neil figured since cats out the bag about Mrs. Arnold and Danny talking, no need to tiptoe around anymore. Tracy has not invited Patrice over here nor has she spoken with her since she saw her at the school. But Neil is hopeful that once she finds out Patrice is a building a relationship with Danny maybe she will come around.

Danny explains they only talk at lunch and how he wishes they can talk more. Neil put his head down and felt even worse. This was all his fault; he shouldn't have kept this a secret for so long knowing they were moving here. He made a mental note to bring that up to Tracy tonight when they talk. "I will talk to your mom son. Don't worry things will get better." Neil got up from the couch to go to the kitchen. "Hey dad" Danny said. "Yeah son" "Grandma said there were some other things I didn't know about, but I will one day. What is she talking about?" Neil just got hot because the pressure is on. Patrice is close to telling Danny about his sister, he can feel it. "Don't worry son. It's all good things."

After dinner Tracy came back downstairs in the kitchen while Neil was washing the dishes. She sat down at the table and Neil dried his hands to sit with her. It was quiet for about 2 mins and then Tracy looked at Neil. "I want you to tell me everything. Do not leave anything out. I have a feeling and part of me is wishing I am wrong." Neil proceeds to tell Tracy absolutely everything.

Danny faked sleep because he wanted to go back into the attic and start reading the papers he had found along with the pictures. He didn't count on his parents being downstairs, but he snuck out his bed anyway. He knows his parents are hiding something because his grandma didn't say what she said for nothing. And his dad response was a dead giveaway.

As Neil is talking, Tracy doesn't know if she should be happy or mad. The more he talked the sicker she felt. Her daughter has been living across the street from her this entire time, she is a student in her classroom, and to put the icing on the cake her husband knew all along. Neil also told her about Mrs. Arnold taking her to church and reporting about her home life. Neil learned how Daniel and his wife do not always keep food in the house. Mrs. Arnold told him how she would save milk for Robbie so their little girl could take it home. Tracy burst into uncontrollable tears.

Upstairs in the attic Danny found a copy of a birth certificate along with adoption papers. Danny recognizes the name, immediately drops the papers and puts his hands over his mouth. He can't believe it; this is what grandma was talking about.

Neil finally got Tracy to calm down and kept apologizing over and over. Tracy was crying for many reasons, the child she had to give up for adoption is alive and well. Tracy never knew how she was doing and had no way to find out. Patrice made sure it was a "closed" adoption. But also made her feel bad for having more kids. The couple she thought were their friends just wanted a check and didn't care about her baby at all. Her child is just being abandoned at every angle. On one hand she is happy Neil kept tabs all of these years but upset he didn't tell her. Now to think of Daniel and Sandy everything just turned red. Sandy knew who she was and never said a word. She came to open house for Rebecca and never even acknowledged they went to school together. Now this forces her to speak with Patrice because she needs to know everything she knows. Tracy mind is made up she will not be going into work tomorrow.

Danny is in disbelief and don't know what to do. Why would his parents lie again? How many other secrets do they have? Does she even know she's adopted? She goes to church with grandma and had no clue? Danny grabs the photos and paperwork and leaves the attic.

Tracy tells Neil they need to come up with a plan to get their little girl home. She wants her back the right legal way. It took everything in Tracy to not go across the street and grab her baby girl. Neil was explaining to Tracy it may not be easy. "So, are you saying we can't get her back?" Tracy asked very upset. "No that's not what I'm trying to say" Neil said. As Danny stood in the kitchen doorway with the papers and photos in his hand he

asked, "So what are you tryna say?"

Chapter 24
Today Was a Good Day

Mama was standing outside when school was over today. I was shocked and surprised to see her because mama never picked me up from school. I didn't know what to think, as soon as I saw her, I asked her if everything was ok. Mama was dressed up; hair was done, and she looked very happy. Now things are getting weird. She is here at school and she's acting like all is well in the world. "Hey baby girl! How was school today?" Mama asked. I gave mama a big hug because it felt good to see her and she wanted to finally see me. "School was meh the usual" I said. "Well how about we go and get something eat and do a little food shopping?" mama asked. "Today is the 12th, there's no check. Did daddy bring you some money?" I asked because I was confused. I was never allowed to go food shopping and mama always says she doesn't have money. "Nope my job gave me some back pay that they owed me" mama said.

"Great! Can I pick out my own cereal? Pllleeeaaassseeeee" I begged. Mama looked at me, grabbed my hand and said, "How about you help me pick out everything we need." I was so excited we skipped down the block for a little bit on our walk home. I dropped off my bookbag and we were right back out the door. Mama had to grab the shopping cart so we can put the bags in there. We went up and down every aisle in the store. Mama let me grab chips, cookies, brownies, and all the new cereals. I wish Robbie was here to enjoy this. I wish mama would have done this before. Why the change all of a sudden? People in the supermarket was staring. A couple of older women told mama they were praying for her. Through it all mama kept a smile on her face.

I really liked this version of mama. On the way home from the supermarket mama said we were going to order Chinese food. She was too tired to cook and had a long day. She asked if I had homework and if I needed any help. I actually didn't have homework and was grateful mama showed she cared. After putting all the food away mama ordered the Chinese food, and we watched movies. We ended up falling asleep on the couch after eating ice cream. Today was a good day.

Chapter 25
I'm Just Thankful

It's been a few weeks and life is great. Mama and I go to church on Sundays with Ms. Arnold. After church Ms. Arnold comes over and mama cooks Sunday dinner. One Sunday Mrs. BlueBridge saw us going into the house, she rushed into her home and closed the door. I don't know if she was upset or not, but Ms. Arnold said not to pay it any mind. She has a lot of skeletons that will be falling out of her closet really soon. When I went to ask her what she meant mama changed the subject. I made a mental note to ask Ms. Arnold when I saw her at school. "So, Thanksgiving is next week. Y'all have any plans?" Ms. Arnold asked. Mama explained to her that it was going to just be me and her. She tried to get daddy to let Robbie come over, but Sandy said no and hung up on mama.

Ms. Arnold said Mr. BlueBridge invited her over there for Thanksgiving. Mama eyes widened and asked if she has spoken to Tracy. How did she know that was Mrs. BlueBridge first name? Ms. Arnold said no and that will be the first time in a few years they will speak. Aside from them seeing each other at school. "You know you guys should really come. It would be great to know what it's like to be around family" Ms. Arnold said. Mama declined the invite again and said she will start cooking. Mama seemed very annoyed with Ms. Arnold and changed the subject. The house phone rang, and it was Serenity. Mama said I could go over there and come back when dinner was done. I grabbed my jacket and ran out the door. I was 2 houses away from Serenity house and I saw Robbie and daddy.

I ran across the street and gave Robbie a hug. Daddy pulled us apart and asked me where I was going. I told him Serenity house and mama was cooking dinner. "Cooking? Ha! I know y'all don't have much ever since I left. It's not the 1st and I didn't give her any money" daddy said. I told daddy mama job gave her back pay that was owed to her. "Back pay huh? You have on new shoes too?" "Yeah! You like them?" I asked as I spun around. "I love them" Robbie said. Daddy said mama probably got them from a John. I have no idea who John is. I looked up at the window and saw Ms. Sandy looking at us. She walked away and came outside when our eyes met. Mrs. Brownstone came out on her porch, saw me talking to daddy and walked over. "Hey Daniel, how are you? Hey Robbie! Sandy" Mrs. Brownstone said with sarcasm. She came out looking for me because she knows it doesn't take that long to walk over to her house. I gave Robbie a hug and told him I will see him later. Ms. Sandy pulled daddy away when I walked over to him. Mrs.

Brownstone pulled me back and said let's go.

I ran over to Serenity's house while Mrs. Brownstone was still talking to daddy. "You know it's 1 thing to wanna have the truth come out and y'all be this 1 big happy family. But to treat her the way you are is disgusting" Mrs. Brownstone told Daniel and Sandy. Sandy stepped closer to Mrs. Brownstone and said "She has a family that's right across the street from her. I had to sit back in the shadows while they played house. You know how it is to have your man step out on you right? Difference is, he hasn't left you for a whole new family…..yet" Sandy said as she walked away. Mrs. Brownstone wanted to slap Sandy to next year for hitting below the belt. "Nice seeing you, come on Robbie" Daniel said as he brushed past Mrs. Brownstone to catch up to Sandy. Mrs. Brownstone walked to her house holding back the tears of the truth Sandy just reminded her of.

Sandy entered the grocery store, looked at Daniel, and said "You sure we have enough? Checks have been bouncing and we cannot survive from the checks you get for her. You said she had millions in that account. What happened?" Daniel wasn't sure what happened, the checks that were being written for "Robbie school" were bouncing, and when Daniel called the bank, he couldn't get any information. "We will be fine; I will figure out what's going on" Daniel reassured Sandy. "Well fix it and fix it fast. Now they have food in the house. She had on a new pair of shoes. Where is she getting money from?" Sandy asked angrily. Daniel always said he would take care of Sandy and he has been up until about 2 weeks ago the money has been drying out.

Serenity was telling me all about her week at school. I haven't been over here for dinner ever since mama has been cooking. I was playing in her hair as she was telling me about the new boy at her school. We went in the kitchen to get something to drink, and I told her about the Thanksgiving invitation. Mrs. Brownstone got up from the couch and asked if we were going. I told her mama declined the offer, but Ms. Arnold was pressing for us to come. Mrs. Brownstone said Ms. Arnold was probably pressing the issue for good reason. I don't see how it would be for good reasoning. It's just my teachers house with her family. Mama and I are getting an invite because they probably feel bad for us. I prefer for it to be just mama and I. Things have been different lately in a great way and I'm just thankful.

Chapter 26
Not Here Not Now

The whole town is getting ready for Christmas and there are decorations everywhere. Thanksgiving was just last week and already people are singing Christmas carols on the corners. Mama went to Kmart and Bradlees to put some stuff on layaway. The community center in town, always hosts a big Christmas dinner for everyone in the town. People would purchase gifts and put them under the tree. The mayor gives the gifts out to all the kids in town that attends the dinner. Mama and daddy always get Robbie and I gift and put it under our tree at home. We weren't allowed to open it until Christmas. Mama and I are gonna put the tree up tomorrow, along with Christmas shopping, she is picking up decorations for the tree.

While mama is gone, I am under the care of Mrs. Brownstone as usual. Serenity was out with her grandma, but I am like her 2nd daughter, so she never minds me coming over. Mrs. Brownstone asked me if mama and I ever talked about what happened. Come to think about it we didn't. It seems like life just went on and got better. "You 2 should definitely talk about it and maybe you can get an understanding of some things." "What is there to try to understand? Robbie's real mom is Ms. Sandy, and we share a dad…… I think" I didn't sound so sure myself. Truth, is I have a lot of questions and just don't want to ruin the mood. Mama has been so happy lately and I am scared to make her upset again. "Maybe 1 day I will ask mama a few questions that I would like to know the answers too" I said.

The phone rang and it was mama. She was back and told me to come home so we can get ready for the towns Christmas dinner. "I will see you tonight at dinner Mrs. Brownstone" I said as I closed the door. Mrs. Brownstone picked up the phone and dialed a number. "Hey, she just walked out the door. When are you going to tell her everything? For Gods sakes the lady is her teacher, and her grandma is her lunch aid." Mrs. Brownstone listened to the voice on the other line before she said, "Ok I am here for whatever you need" and hung up. Mrs. Brownstone thought to herself these secrets are getting out of hand. She doesn't know how much longer she can hold it in. Serenity walked in and interrupted her mom's thoughts. "Hey mom I'm back" Serenity shouted. Mrs. Brownstone looked at her and said, "Sit down, there's something I wanna tell you."

Mama and I are getting ready for the towns Christmas dinner. The phone rings and mama answered it. "Yes, that will be fine. Trust me I will be ok. I just want to get this over with. Thank you for everything, ok see you soon bye". I was in my room but heard everything, who was mama talking too? I would dial *69 to see who called but I don't know anyone's phone number besides Serenity.

Neil hung up the phone and fixed his tie. Danny was standing in the doorway. "Dad who was that" Danny asked. "A client of mine. I just got an update to their case and wanted to call and give them the good news." "You know we are going to see her at the dinner tonight? How long are we going to keep this up? She deserves to know we are her real family! If you and mom don't tell her. I will." Danny stormed off holding back tears. He just can't understand why his parents are hiding so many things. He feels like he doesn't even know who they are anymore.

Tracy walked in the room after the chaos and had a confused looked on her face. Neil caught her up on what just happened, and Tracy admitted she is growing impatient too. Neil reassures her, he is handling it and the time is coming to bring their little girl home. Danny folds the birth certificate and a couple of photos in his pocket. "I'm going to tell her tonight when I see her" Danny thought to himself. He was done waiting.

As soon as you walk in you can hear the Christmas music playing. "Silent Night" by The Temptations, "Have Yourself a Merry Little Christmas" by Luther Vandross. Mama and I wore matching red dresses. I had half of my hair up in a ponytail with curls on the ends and the back of my hair was out with curls. Mama put a relaxer in her hair with a bun in the back and curls. Everyone started coming in, Serenity and her family, Jane and her family, Danny and his family, and Rebecca walked in with her new family. I immediately felt sick, daddy wasn't too nice to me the other day. He walked over to mama and said hi. He proceeded to ask her how many times she laid on her back to look this good. Mama said as many times as Sandy and walked away. Serenity and I looked at each other with our mouths open.

Rebecca came over to say hi but couldn't stay long. Ms. Sandy told her they had to stay together as a family. She looked so sad and couldn't hang with her friends. Danny ran over to me and grab my arm to pull me to the side. "Hey, there is something I've been meaning to tell you" Serenity walked over and said "Girl I need to borrow you for a second. I gotta unload this information I got, to you."

"Well sorry Serenity, this information is really important" Serenity cut Danny off and said, "Well sorry to burst your bubble but this is very important." The mayor tapped the glass with a spoon and interrupted our conversation. It was time for the yearly speech. While the mayor was speaking these men burst through the door. "Everyone calm down and have a seat. We are looking for Sandy

Whitegrass and David Blackbird." They walked over to daddy and said, "David Blackbird you are under arrest for fraud." The cops were putting hand cuffs on daddy and mama had a smirk on her face. "Sandy Whitegrass, you have been served." Ms. Sandy was being sued by MAMA!

Ms. Sandy looked at mama and said "Oh so you think you won? All of that money you have, and you still chose to live the way you did! You owed me! You stole my man, so I had to get my revenge!" Mama walked over to Ms.

Sandy and said, "And now I am getting mine." Mama walked over to daddy while the officer was reading him his rights. "After all of these years, you really thought I would never find out y'all were writing checks from that account and Robbie doesn't go to a *special school*. See what you didn't know is that there was a clause in the money. Spouses did not have access to the money. So y'all forged my signature but you missed the yearly letter that comes in the mail to confirm all transactions were accurate. Yeah, see I checked the mail too. I contacted the bank and set up an appointment. I went in and provided my signature and started an investigation."

Everyone was frozen and silent. No one knew what to say. Mama walked over to her purse and grabbed some papers. She folded them and put them in daddy back pocket. They were divorce papers. Ms. Sandy walked over to me pointing her finger in my face and said "Enjoy your little moment now. Because your world is about to come crashing down." Mrs. BlueBridge jumped in Ms. Sandy face and said, "Touch my child and I will mop this floor with you" Mr. BlueBridge grabbed

Mrs. BlueBridge and said, "Not here, not now".

Chapter 27
What About Me

"Don't touch my child. Don't touch my child" is all I kept replaying in my head. Why would Mrs. BlueBridge say that? Mama didn't correct her either, heck NO ONE corrected her. THIS! This is what Danny wanted to tell me! I'm surrounded by everyone and again the walls are closing in. My feet are planted, and I can't move. Mama, Mrs. Brownstone, Ms. Arnold, Mrs. BlueBridge,

Serenity, Jane, and Danny are all talking to me, but I don't hear anything. I see Ms. Sandy leaving with Robbie and Rebecca and I still can't form any sound to leave my lips. I feel a chair in the back of my legs, and I take a seat. The dinner was over, and people were leaving. Serenity brought me a cup of water, but I didn't want it. What I want is questions answered.

"I'm sorry you found out this way. I was trying to tell you. Here look at this" Danny handed me so folded papers and photos. It's my birth certificate! With

Tracy and Neil as my parents! "Danny! Where did you get that from?" Mrs. BlueBridge asked in confusion, taking the papers away from me. "Mom she already knows! Thanks to you blurting it out in front of everyone! There's a box in the attic with all these photos and papers" Danny barked at Mrs. BlueBridge. While they were talking mama came over and knelt in front of me with tears coming down her face. "I'm so sorry baby. I have completely failed you." At this point I am crying; things were going great with just me and mama. I no longer wanted to know if it was true, she wasn't my birth mom. I didn't care because for once she cared and I was happy again. "Mama is it true? Is Mr. and Mrs. BlueBridge my birth parents?"

Mama nodded yes and gave me a hug and all my tears were flowing. I heard Mrs. Brownstone say to Serenity to get her things. Once I let mama go, I saw Mrs. BlueBridge and Ms. Arnold standing side by side. I stood up and told mama I was ready to go. I had nothing to say to either of them. Ms. Arnold knew my struggles and never said anything. I am in Mrs. BlueBridge class, and she pretended to not know me. All the hurt was turning into rage. How long did Danny know? What was it Serenity tried to tell me? Did she know too? Everyone lied to me, and I do not trust anyone.

Mama told the story how she went to Mr. BlueBridge office, filed the paperwork for divorce, and the claims against daddy and Ms. Sandy. Mr. BlueBridge gave her some money until the account was unfrozen. In the meantime, she had no access to her account until her case was closed. I need to see Robbie and be there for him. I don't care what Ms. Sandy says she doesn't know Robbie like I do. Opal and Whitney ran to me excited they had an older sister. Mr. and Mrs. BlueBridge walked over to me and just stood there. "I am so sorry I embarrassed you like this. This isn't how I wanted us to meet again. When I put all the pieces together and realized who you were, I couldn't hold it in" Mrs. BlueBridge explained.

"There is so much that must be explained to you. If you give us a chance, we would like to sit down and tell you everything" Mr. BlueBridge pleaded.

"Yeah, I would like that. I have a lot of questions for everyone. I'm gonna use the bathroom and go home with mama. I am tired, excuse me" I said as I walked past them. It pained Mrs. BlueBridge to hear her daughter call someone else mama. Something she is finally admitting out loud.

I went to use the bathroom and heard 2 voices come in the bathroom. I recognized them right away. I didn't leave the stall because I wanted to hear what they were saying. As soon as I heard my name my ears perked up right away. "I am so glad this came to light. There is so much more she doesn't know, and I hope they tell her everything." "Yeah, but 1 step at a time, that poor girl been through a lot." "Yeah, but that Sandy is a trip. She has been on Daniels heels since high school." "If they don't tell her everything about herself I will." I walked out the stall and saw Ms. Arnold and Mrs. Brownstone and they look like they saw a ghost. I looked at them and said, "Since we are all here and you know so much about everyone, WHAT ABOUT ME?"